A LONG TIME AGO
Growing up with and out of STAR WARS

GIB VAN ERT

Soi-disant press

Trade paper: ISBN-13: 978-0-9881180-0-3
Kindle: ISBN 978-0-9881180-1-0
ePub: ISBN 978-0-9881180-2-7

First published August 2012. This edition July 2013.

"I'm getting too old for this sort of thing."
Obi-Wan Kenobi, *Star Wars* (1977)

CONTENTS

ACKNOWLEDGMENTS

I am indebted to the following people in getting this book together. Mistakes in grammar, punctuation and judgment remain my own: Gary Collinson; Theo Colombo; Greg Moore; Nash; Christopher Schuld; David Spratley; Michael Van Ert; Cassandra Whalen; Wayne Ziants. Thanks also to my sister April for her support and encouragement, my mother for her unquestioning faith in the brilliance of all my half-baked ideas, and my wife Stephanie for, well, EVERYTHING.

STARING AT SKYWALKER

I remove a heavy diaper from around my son's waist. It is the environmentally friendly kind—biodegradable, with a reusable liner and cloth portion, as expensive as it is ineffective. Before our daughter was born my wife and I had strong feelings about the subject. But Beatrice is two and half now, Zachary is ten weeks, and I am well past caring about diapers in landfills. I put on a proper diaper. I will make up the environmental damage elsewhere. I'll decline plastic cutlery when I buy lunch.

Oblivious of landfills and cutlery, Zachary stares at the picture hanging on the wall above his change table. He has been looking at it for a few weeks now—about as long as he has been physically capable of focusing on anything. Every diaper change, he studies the comicbook colours, the human—or at least

1

humanoid—forms, the joined up lettering that is nothing like handwriting. He does not know what he is seeing, except perhaps that it is what his sister calls Skywalker. Every diaper change, Zach contemplates Skywalker.

He is looking at six Marvel *Star Wars* comics, arranged three by two on a sky blue matte and framed under glass. I got the idea about ten years ago while watching an episode of *Buffy the Vampire Slayer*. The man at the art shop offered me museum-quality glass but it was more expensive and I had duplicates of these issues. When they faded I would replace them from my collection, or pick up more from the comic book shop. No one seemed to want them anymore anyway.

Not that *Star Wars* had quit being popular. "Popular" is too mild a word. *Star Wars* was then and remains now the ubiquitous moneychurning steamrolling blockbuster entertainment phenomenon of modern times. But Marvel *Star Wars* comics were not that kind of *Star Wars*. Looking at these comic books, especially the early ones, children who learned about Darth Maul before Darth Vader would not know if they were Buck Rogers or Flash Gordon. They are beyond outmoded; they are antiquarian. And that, in part, is why I framed them and hung the resulting piece prominently on one of the only four walls in my bachelor apartment a decade ago. Also because I thought it was funny. Probably also because it was cool in the "retro" way that was becoming fashionable at the time. But what I liked most about my framed Marvel *Star Wars* comics was the contrast between them and the *Star Wars* that had come since. At a time when the "prequels" were playing in theatres to packed houses and critical scorn, this was the *Star Wars* of my childhood.

That is not as naïve as it sounds. I am not suggesting that there was a time when a movie called *Star Wars* appeared in cinemas unsullied by ad men and marketing campaigns. I know that *Star Wars* was never free of exuberant commercialization, principally in the form of rampant product tie-ins; as a boy I literally bathed in them. But in retrospect there are differences. The *Star Wars* of my childhood, from 1977 to about 1985, had at times an awkwardness, even a clumsiness, about it that is now entirely gone. Like its biggest fans, *Star Wars* then was young and new.

Star Wars—the movie, the sequels, the toys, the books, the trading cards, the comics, the arcade games, the galaxy of myths and merchandise—dominated my youth. In this I am the same as so many other boys I knew then, and so many men I know today. It is a common reference point for my gender and generation. Yet there was a time before *Star Wars*, and I was born into it. When I first saw the film, at a long-gone drive-in theatre in Penticton, British Columbia, sitting in the back seat of a station wagon my father borrowed from the car dealership he worked at, as I watched the opening words float across the giant screen unable to read them but thrilled by their movement, as the exhilarating score filled the car through clumsy, tinny speakers hanging off the rolled-down front windows, as all this washed over me for the very first time, I had no idea what was coming. I did not know about lightsabers or stormtroopers or jawas or droids. Nobody did.

Watching my son stare at Skywalker while I change his diaper it occurs to me that for him it will be completely different. Whatever attraction it may hold for him, *Star Wars* will not come with surprise or wonder or astonishment. It will be a part of his cultural horizon before he even sees the films. It will be like the picture on his bedroom wall—a furnishing. Reflecting on this, I think for a moment that I should take the picture down. But it would not help. *Star Wars* is everywhere.

*

If you ask its original fans, meaning me and the millions of others around the world who grew up with it, *Star Wars* has lost its way. I do not know anyone in his or her late 30s or early 40s who feels much attachment to *Star Wars* as it re-emerged in 1999 with *The Phantom Menace*. On the contrary, complaining about the detested prequels has become as much a part of the *Star Wars* experience for my generation today as raving about the original films was when we were ten-year-olds. But whether *Star Wars* has gone off the rails or not, it remains a runaway train that shows no signs of stopping. If it does keep going, and maybe even if it does not, some account of the phenomenon should be attempted—not just by critics or industry insiders but by those of us who made *Star Wars* what it is today. Some description of its appeal—initially as a film but quickly thereafter as a pop culture phenomenon—should be offered to the parents, spouses and now the children of this first *Star Wars* generation.

I am as qualified to give such an account as anyone, although I do not claim to be the world's biggest *Star Wars* fan. I cannot recite any of the films from memory, though I do have quite a few of the lines down. I do not have an especially large or valuable collection of *Star Wars* memorabilia, but there are six boxes of toys and mementos, most worn from use, carefully stored away in my basement. I cannot bring myself to part with them. I have never attended any sort of convention or *Star-Wars*-themed social event. I did dress up as Luke

Skywalker for Halloween in 2003, but that was as much laziness as ardour; it makes a pretty easy costume if you have a lightsaber (I did) and a karate jacket (which I borrowed). If I am qualified to give an account of *Star Wars*'s youth, it is because I shared it with my own. I offer myself not as an expert but as a participant and eyewitness.

The *Star Wars* phenomenon cannot be explained entirely by the quality of the films. In saying so I am not disparaging the original trilogy. *Star Wars* regularly appears on film critic lists, often standing out amongst more intellectual or literary entries. *The Empire Strikes Back* and *Return of the Jedi* do not always receive the same treatment, but all three films are nonetheless marvellous instances of cinematic storytelling. But there must be something more to *Star Wars*. People do not dress up as *Citizen Kane* characters on Halloween. Children do not ask their parents for *Lawrence of Arabia* action figures for Christmas. Lego does not sell *La Dolce Vita* playsets. These comparisons may seem facile but they underscore the extent to which *Star Wars* has imposed itself upon our culture in a way that other successful or highly regarded films have not. Clearly the massive marketing edifice that grew up in response to the staggering commercial success of *Star Wars* is part of the explanation for the *Star Wars* phenomenon. But it can only be part. Dozens of so-called blockbuster movies are released every year, supported by enormous promotional campaigns flooding media outlets, fast food restaurants and toy stores with advertisements and product tie-ins. Yet even those that are considered successful do not come close to penetrating popular culture the way *Star Wars* has.

So what is it? What is it about *Star Wars* that left such an imprint on me and my generation, particularly its boys? How did a film become a phenomenon? In the pages that follow I attempt, from time to time, some explanation. But ultimately the only account I can give of *Star Wars* is a personal one. It starts as a four-year-old. It is inextricably bound up in my particular experiences: my home town, my sister, my grandparents, my best friend, my adolescence and young adulthood. Despite its worldwide notoriety, *Star Wars* is in many ways a private matter for me.

This book therefore takes the form of a memoir, with personalities and incidents peculiar to my experience. But I am far from being the only person who could tell such a story. Despite the commonplace depiction of *Star Wars* today as a 'geek' or 'nerd' interest—what do those words mean anymore in a world where formerly marginal interests like computing and science fiction have gone entirely mainstream?—the original three films swept up, in varying degrees, children of all kinds, all over the world. While the details are my own, an entire generation of *Star-Wars*-mad children, now entering middle age, lived this story's broad outlines.

[STAR WARS]
ASLEEP AT THE DRIVE-IN

On an unremarkable day in February 1972 the people who would become my mother and father drove a pale blue Volkswagen van north along Washington State Route 9 to the Sumas border crossing and asked to be let in. Neither of them had ever been to Canada. Now they were about to take refuge there, though they did not tell the border guard that. Their immediate cause for flight was the Vietnam War. But for my mother, a Texas beauty queen turned hippy, this was more than political. By running away with my father she was abandoning a life of privilege, prudery and prejudice which seemed natural to her as an 18-year-old Dallas socialite in 1960 but had become oppressive by the early 1970s. Her departure was a bid for liberation. My father's flight motive was more stark. He had been away without leave from his marine corps base at Camp Lejeune, North Carolina for over a year. He had spent the time travelling around the United States, seeing the sights like any other tourist, without ever being detected by the authorities. But he knew it was only a matter of time. When captured he could expect a court martial, a fate worse than Canada. So shortly after meeting each other at a drug rehabilitation clinic (they tell me they were volunteering there), my parents headed north. They told the man at the checkpoint they were visiting friends. In fact they were about to become asylum-seekers, uncertain when or even if they would ever go home.

Based on this story, I have sometimes told people that I am the child of immigrants, even refugees. While it is effectively true, I mean it as a sort of joke. Refugees and other immigrants are common here, and I do not fit their usual description. I am white, a native English speaker and generally indistinguishable from the bred-in-the-bone Canadian boys I went to school with, boys with names like Gordie McAlpine and Dave Sawchuk. Yet growing up I did sometimes sense a difference between me and them. For any immigrant, Canada is an easy place to surround oneself with reminders of the old country. This is especially true when the old country is the United States of the 1970s, with its movies, magazines and even television stations constantly threatening (unintentionally) to drown out any native popular culture. No doubt this was part of the attraction of Canada for US draft dodgers; it was nearly home. For much of their first ten years or so in Canada, my parents showed little interest in their adopted country. My mother liked Gordon Lightfoot, and was intrigued by how British Canada was, with its Royal Mail boxes (now gone), coats of arms and unfamiliar holidays: Victoria Day, Dominion Day, Remembrance Day, Boxing Day. My father quickly became a fan of the Vancouver Canucks. But, initially at least, that was about as Canadian as my parents got. They watched US newscasts every evening and the *Today Show* in the mornings, so that what little I knew about public affairs by the time I was school age concerned a foreign country. The result was that I embarrassed myself in class by not knowing the names of Canadian leaders, the capitals of Canadian provinces, or even the names of the provinces themselves. Thanks to my non-immigrant appearance—in those days you could generally tell immigrants from natives by their appearance—my ignorance of these basics made me look stupid when in fact I was just a little foreign.

My parents found Canadian hippy friends sympathetic to US draft dodgers in Vancouver. I was born there in 1973. My sister followed two years later, and shortly after that our family moved to Cranbrook, a small town in eastern British Columbia. We did not stay long, and all I remember of the place is that the doors of our house had hooks on their bottoms that fitted into matching eyelets on the adjoining walls to hold them open. While Cranbrook is but a single, random memory to me, the next town we moved to, in early 1977, was the scene of most of my childhood.

Geographically, Penticton, British Columbia is far from what my parents must have imagined when they escaped to Canada. It sits just north of the northern edge of the Sonoran Desert, a climatic zone reaching all the way to Mexico. As a boy walking in the hills south of town I was more likely to tread in cactus than snow, more likely to startle a rattlesnake than a beaver. Resting at the tip of this arid ecosystem, Penticton is something of an oasis, surrounded by orchards and nestled between two large lakes with sandy beaches. Growing up I assumed every town had a beach or two. Every town I knew did: Penticton, Summerland, Peachland, Oliver, Osoyoos, even Kelowna.

My parents rented half of a duplex on a cul-de-sac called Highland Place, up Carmi Mountain. This was just about the eastern edge of human settlement in Penticton. When I got old enough to explore on my bike, I discovered that there were no more houses three

12

or four blocks east: just bluish-green pine trees against the dry hillside. In summer I spent the hot days catching grasshoppers in tin coffee cans. I would sneak up on one, drop the can over it upside-down, slip a plastic lid underneath to seal it in, poke a few breathing holes in the lid with a nail, listen to it bang around in its tin prison for a while, then release it and go in search of a better prize. In the evenings children emerged from the houses around the cul-de-sac dragging out goalie nets and hockey sticks. We played until it was too dark to see the tennis ball. Winters were what my parents must have expected from Canada. Snow covered everything I could see from our single-pane living room window: the hill, the pine trees, the boxy, plain duplexes huddled around the cul-de-sac, the cars frozen in gravel driveways.

*

On 25 May 1977, shortly after our arrival in Penticton, *Star Wars* was released upon an unsuspecting world. I have briefly described my first encounter with the film at the local drive-in. At about the point at which the rebels are preparing their assault on the Death Star—perhaps 10 p.m.—I fell asleep. But that is no slight against the movie. I was four years old; it was impossible for me to do otherwise. That I made it as far along as that is a wonder. My early impressions of the film are mostly indistinct. They have blurred over time with reactions to countless subsequent viewings and also with later, clearer recollections of my responses to the two sequels. Besides this, all my earliest childhood memories are shadowy at the edges, and I often cannot say with certainty what is a true recollection and what is reconstructed from later information.

But I am confident in my memory of the opening sequence of *Star Wars*. Has another movie ever started so well? First came the fairy tale opening line, written not spoken, as if from a storybook: A long time ago in a galaxy far, far away... Then the crash of the orchestra and the yellow *Star Wars* logo against space blackness. The music was thrillingly confident, unhesitatingly proclaiming to the filmgoer that he was about to see something unlike anything he had seen before. Then the opening text, again spelled out without narration, the words floating away from the viewer and into deep space until indecipherable. I did not know what the words said but the music and visuals carried me along. The total effect was exhilaratingly new yet deeply familiar: I was about to be told a grand story.

Once the yellow words have receded into nothingness and the music has dropped, the camera pans down to reveal a moon, then another, and then the hazy atmosphere of a planet. Against this backdrop a ship races across space chased by bursts of laser fire. Next its pursuer appears at the top of the screen. It looks larger than the ship it chases, then much larger, then larger still. Its underside comes to fill the screen. The thing is a monster. Our sympathy moves firmly to its quarry. The massive spacecraft overtakes its prey and draws it into its belly like a whale swallowing a minnow. Meanwhile, inside the doomed vessel, its crew of soldiers, robots and even (it is said) a princess prepare to be boarded. The soldiers wear simple, even casual uniforms. Their only armour consists of large white helmets, the open fronts of which reveal apprehensive yet determined faces.

The soldiers take their places along a white corridor ending in a sealed door. They must know the door will not hold. They train their weapons on it expectantly. The door breaks, then explodes. Through it pour white, armour-clad troops, each just like the one that came before. The ensuing firefight brings losses to both sides, but the invading force is too numerous. The resistance falls back, then routs.

Then through the exploded portal comes a figure some seven feet high and clad entirely in black, from his menacingly-helmeted head to the cloak that covers his shoulders and trails along the floor behind him. Like the stormtroopers who stand to attention as he passes by, this figure might at first be mistaken for something mechanic. His eyes, face and body are completely covered in armour, so there is no knowing what it might conceal. Yet his movements are fluid and natural, completely unlike those of the two robots we saw moments earlier making their way improbably through the crossfire. Most tellingly, the black giant breathes, inhaling and exhaling audibly as he surveys the wreckage he has brought. In some corrupt way, this dark invader is human.

These opening moments of *Star Wars* imprinted themselves on my memory from the start. In a span of minutes they communicated all the film's themes: space, adventure, oppression, resistance, machinery and humanity. I was enthralled. I was not alone.

*

I need hardly say that *Star Wars* was an astonishingly popular and profitable movie. Today it is sometimes said to have been surpassed, financially at least, by more recent blockbusters ("*Shrek 2* made more money than *Star Wars*!"). But that is fatuous. It is only the difference between the $15 ticket prices we pay today and the $2.50 our parents paid in 1977. Nor was the film a merely local phenomenon. It was translated into every major language, from Arabic to Vietnamese, and succeeded to varying degrees everywhere it went. When worldwide inflation-adjusted figures are added to the staggering US draw, *Star Wars* becomes undisputedly the most commercially successful movie ever made—even before factoring in profits from the film's countless product tie-ins, from t-shirts to toys, breakfast cereal to bubble bath.

Commercial success on an unprecedented scale was no doubt a surprise to everyone concerned with the film. Among those caught particularly flatfooted, however, was Kenner Products, the Cincinnati toy company that obtained the rights to produce *Star Wars* toys before the film was released and after rival Mego Corporation passed up the opportunity. While Kenner had the foresight to purchase rights Mego had declined, it must not have valued them very highly for it made no arrangements to bring *Star Wars* action figures to market in time for the 1977 holiday season. There was, of course, no shortage of other kinds of *Star Wars* merchandise available by late 1977, much of it produced by Kenner. But action figures were the pinnacle of any serious merchandising campaign directed at boys. An action figure is really just a doll, but boys supposedly do not play with dolls and so the phrase "action figure" was coined. The first action figure, G.I. Joe, was a plastic, eight-inch-high, articulated and posable doll with interchangeable outfits and accessories—a Barbie for boys. Hasbro and Mego Corporation were the leading action figure producers in the 1960s and mid '70s. In the late 1970s a Japanese toymaker, Takara, introduced a new form factor, the 3¾ inch figurine, apparently in response to rising plastic prices. When Kenner finally brought *Star Wars* action figures to market in 1978, it mostly adopted this smaller format. Action figures have been this size ever since.

By the time Kenner could see how much money it was about to make from its *Star Wars* licence, it was too late to get figures moulded, tested, packaged and shipped to the shops in time for Christmas. Scrambling for a way to cash in on the emerging craze at the peak of the toy-buying season, Kenner devised an elaborate rain cheque which it called the Early Bird Certificate Package. The naming of this scheme was a typical bit of ad man dissembling: in the face of its potentially devastating tardiness to market, Kenner shamelessly told the public that it was not late, we were just early. The Early Bird Certificate Package consisted of a display stand (against which to display action figures that did not yet exist), a *Star Wars* club card ("You didn't get any *Star Wars* figures for Christmas? Join the club"), a few stickers, and a certificate which the recipient could mail away in exchange for four action figures, once they were ready: Luke Skywalker, Princess Leia, R2-D2 and Chewbacca.

I do not remember much of the Christmas of 1977, but my mother tells me I did not receive an Early Bird Certificate Package. I did get some sort of *Star-Wars*-related gift—I believe it was Kenner's Escape from Death Star board game. It was not until next Christmas, 1978, that *Star Wars* fully transformed itself from a movie I had enjoyed but fallen asleep watching to a prolonged, unrelenting, toy-and-other-merchandise-fuelled childhood obsession. For this my maternal grandparents were heavily responsible. We spent the holidays in Penticton that year. My grandparents were not there. In fact they did not visit Canada at all after my sister's birth in 1975. In their place they sent presents, including two large giftwrapped boxes, one for me and one for my sister. I have a distinct recollection of these two boxes. Their size and similarity intrigued me, as did the shuffling sound they made when shaken. (My mother had put these and other presents under the tree many days before Christmas, and I had made a careful inspection of each, weighing and shaking them in an effort to guess their contents.) When finally on Christmas morning it came time to open the twin boxes, my sister and I tore into them at the same time. Both contained blister pack after blister pack of Kenner *Star Wars* action figures. I cannot say how many. It seemed like hundreds, but by Christmas 1978 Kenner was only making about 20 figures so it must have been no more than a dozen. In any case it was a lot. I was ecstatic. My sister was also very pleased, but looking back and considering how her interests developed in later years I think she liked these toys mainly because her big brother liked them, and she liked him.

The Christmas of 1978 was the first for me in which *Star Wars* was the main attraction. My every Christmas after that for the next seven years was dominated by toys and other merchandise relating to the movie and its sequels. We were not religious people in any orthodox way and so the meaning of the holiday as a spiritual or historical occasion never mattered to me. Until some time after *Return of the Jedi* came out, Christmas was, as far as I knew or cared, a purely secular occasion dedicated to increasing the bulk of my considerable collection of *Star Wars* memorabilia with the latest plastic allurements devised by Lucasfilm and Kenner.

From the perspective of the toymakers and marketing types at Kenner, my sister and I were nearly an exact fit: "Ages four and up" was how they put it on their packaging, and by Christmas 1978 that is about what we were. By this time Kenner had got its act together and filled the toy stores of the western world with *Star Wars* action figures. Kenner made other *Star Wars* toys, too, but all that ever mattered to me were the action figures and their accompanying playsets and vehicles. Kenner's initial run consisted of twelve figures: Luke Skywalker, Chewbacca, Princess Leia Organa and R2-D2 (the four "early bird" figures) plus Darth Vader, Ben (Obi Wan) Kenobi, Han Solo, C-3PO, Stormtrooper, Jawa, Sand People and Death Squad Commander.

How this last figure ever made it on to toy store shelves is beyond me. The name alone was reason enough for any sensible parent to refuse to buy it. How is a Death Squad Commander a proper gift for a child of any age, never mind a four-year-old? Unless you live in the Third Reich, how do you explain to your wife that you bought the boy a couple of Stormtroopers and a Death Squad Commander for his birthday? Eventually someone must have realized that this was not a good name for a children's toy, for Kenner rebranded the figure as Star Destroyer Commander. But changing the name did not make the figure itself any less pointless. This was surely the worst figure Kenner ever made. It was based on a few uniformed extras—you cannot call them characters as they have no lines in the film and almost no significance to the plot—shown fleetingly on a few unremarkable occasions during the Death Star sequences. The Kenner figurine is dressed in black boots (what self-respecting death squad commander would wear anything else?), a large black helmet and a grey pyjama-style uniform which is inconsistent with the film (where they were dressed in black) and, more importantly, totally stupid looking. I was mystified by this figure. What was I supposed to do with it? When I think now that it took a spot that could have gone to the rebel troopers shown in the film's opening sequence, or to Grand Moff Tarkin—both characters for which Kenner never made figures—I am baffled.

But there were many more hits than misses in these original twelve figurines. Kenobi, Vader, Chewbacca, Threepio, Artoo, Stormtrooper, Sand People—these were all superb. Threepio must have been the most successful likeness from the film, really beautifully done. Artoo's head clicked when you turned it—possibly the only sound Artoo did not make in the film, but still a great effect. For sheer pleasure, the Chewbacca figurine was my pick. His rifle did not much resemble the weapon Chewbacca actually carried in the movie, but it was still the best accessory Kenner made. Darth Vader and Obi-Wan Kenobi were captivating. I spent hours duelling with them. Princess Leia came with a slender blaster unlike any of the weapons the other figures sported. For every figure, it seemed, Kenner knew to add a special touch.

There were nevertheless some peculiarities in the original figurines. Han Solo, for instance, came in two versions: one with a disproportionately small head and the other with a disproportionately large one. The heads were not just different sizes but different sculpts altogether. The larger head had bangs covering Han's forehead and lines under his eyes. The effect was of a tired boy, or a middle-aged man trying to look young. I had Big Head Han (the more common of the two) and was always unhappy with him.

I was also ambivalent about the telescoping lightsabers built into the right arms of Vader, Kenobi and Luke. "Telescoping" is the term collectors have coined. It means that the lightsaber was thick for the most part but thinner at the end. To make the figure draw his lightsaber, you pushed the handle (tucked behind the back of its right shoulder) down, ejecting the saber from the hollow arm. I disliked this arrangement even as a five-year-old. It meant that the figure's right hand could never hold anything else, and the left hand was sculpted so that it couldn't either—at least not well. Plus, even when the lightsaber was fully retracted its thin tip stuck out, as if the character perpetually had his weapon on butter-knife-mode. This made no sense, and usually resulted in the tip breaking off altogether. Beyond all this, Kenner's telescoping lightsabers were inconsistent with my memories of the film—supported by images I found in books, on trading cards and elsewhere—in which lightsabers were the same thickness from top to bottom. All of this was annoying to me even as a small boy. When, in 1980, Kenner released its Luke Skywalker in Bespin Fatigues figure, it dumped the telescoping lightsaber in favour of a separate, non-telescoping weapon that could be placed in and removed from the figure's hand. I considered this a vast improvement, and kept hoping Kenner would remake Vader and Obi-Wan the same way. They never did.

Kenner later added eight more figures to its *Star Wars* line-up: Death Star Droid, Greedo, Hammerhead, Snaggletooth, Walrus Man, Luke Skywalker X-Wing Pilot, Power Droid and R5-D4. The pick of this bunch was easily the X-Wing Pilot: Luke in his bright orange flight suit and white helmet with those curious markings which were to become the recognized insignia of the rebel forces. I also liked the colourful, alien forms of Greedo and Hammerhead. But I did not really get much play out of most of these new figures. In retrospect many of them look to me like early instances of Kenner's practice of churning out action figures of doubtful importance to the story of the film. Perhaps the company's experience with Death Squad Commander had taught it that a significant portion of its market would buy any action figure Kenner stuck a *Star Wars* label on, however ridiculous the toy itself.

From the beginning, Kenner's figurines were sold in a form of packaging known as a blister pack. This consisted of a rectangular piece of cardboard with a small hole at the top (for hanging the item on a display rack) and a glued-on piece of transparent plastic in which the figurine was contained. This was positioned in the bottom left corner of the cardboard, leaving about two-thirds of the front of the packaging available for displaying the *Star Wars* logo (which, by 1978, was already iconic) and a large photograph, usually a still from the movie, of the character represented by the figurine. The other side of the blister pack was devoted to promoting Kenner's other action figures and accessories. The contents of these promotions changed frequently but always consisted of a photographic line-up of Kenner's action figures. This way, children like me could drool over the product line and plan our next birthday and Christmas wish lists. The back of the cardstock also invariably featured a small blue and white proof of purchase seal from (strangely) General Mills. Kenner frequently ran promotions inviting children to collect a free figurine by sending four or five proofs-of-purchase in the mail to their address in Ohio. Sometimes these mail-away orders were for figures not yet available in the shops, such as Boba Fett (the first such promotion) and Anakin Skywalker (possibly the last). The Anakin figure, of course, was the smiling white-haired gentleman of the original *Return of the Jedi*, not Hayden Christiansen with a ponytail.

The allure of Kenner's packaging should not be overlooked. It was part of what made *Star Wars* figures so attractive. Blister packs gave children a lot to look at: the figurine itself, encased in its clear plastic shell, but also the large photograph of the character drawn from the film—a film most of us had not seen often and wanted to see again.

These Kenner action figures completely dominated that part of my childhood I actually remember, say from about four-and-a-half to twelve. I had other toys. I liked other things. But *Star Wars* figures obsessed me. When my mother was going through one of her endless flirtations with alternative religious beliefs—in this case Jehovah's Witnesses—she taught my sister and me a bedtime prayer, a recitation in our young minds of all the things we had to be thankful for. My mother suggested we thank Jehovah for mummy and daddy, grandpa and grandma and Re Re (our great-grandmother), and Momma Cat and Muffy (our pet cats). I adopted this list and added to the end of it my *Star Wars* figures. We were not Jehovah's Witnesses for long. Long enough for my sister and me to laugh uncontrollably one Sunday morning at Kingdom Hall when we broke Princess Leia's head off inside a Dewback. Long enough that one of our Christmases was replaced by Family Week—an invention of my mother's to spare us the loss of our favourite holiday by not formally celebrating Christmas (to which Jehovah's Witnesses object) while still exchanging *Star Wars* toys and other presents. This might have mollified some of the parishioners but I doubt Jehovah was fooled by it. It did not matter, however, for my mother moved quickly on to Taoism, then Chinese astrology, then western astrology, then Norse runes, then numerology, all of which I found quite acceptable as they involved no attendance at church and no prohibition of occasions on which gifts were given to children. Long after our stint as Jehovah's Witnesses, however, I kept saying that prayer in my head every night. If there was a god, I wanted him to know how grateful I was for the Kenner toy company of Cincinnati, Ohio.

*

Fanaticism for a film was not easy to feed in the 1970s and early '80s. Today if one wishes to see a movie ten times it is only a matter of calling it up on the screen and setting aside twenty hours or so of one's life for viewing and re-viewing it. In this and other ways technology has facilitated poor judgment. Things were different in the first *Star Wars* era, say from 1977 to 1984. The theatres and drive-ins only showed films for a limited time. Of course there were repertory cinemas in big cities that continued showing films after they had left the first-run houses, but no such cinema existed in Penticton, and probably not within 300 kilometres of it. The free-to-air television channels were few and none secured the rights to show *Star Wars* until 1984, seven years after its release. Home video systems such as VHS and Betamax existed by the late 1970s but they were rare and novel, especially in small-town British Columbia. My family did not get a VCR until the late 1980s. And even if we had wanted, and could have afforded, such a device sooner it would not have given me access to *Star Wars* until the film's first home video release in 1982.

The result was that in the late 1970s I was a *Star Wars* fan who had not seen much of *Star Wars*. Most of my friends were the same. We had all seen it once or twice, rarely more, and those viewings were in 1977 or 1978. We saw nothing more of *Star Wars*, on film at least, until the spring of 1980, when *The Empire Strikes Back* came out. By that time, and well before then, what I knew of *Star Wars* did not come directly from George Lucas's film. That was a faded memory, and an incomplete one at that since I had fallen asleep the first time I saw it, and I did not see it again before 1982. Instead, my knowledge of and devotion to *Star Wars* came from the near endless array of toys, books, soundtracks, television tie-ins, trading cards, board games and other merchandise that came into the orbit of *Star Wars*, like satellites of some fading sun, from 1977 onwards. For about two years, from mid-1978 until the release of *Empire*, *Star Wars* for me ceased to be a movie and became instead a mishmash of popular culture displays referring to it, often rather loosely.

The Kenner toys were what chiefly focussed my mind on *Star Wars* in this period, but they were not all. Everyone who could possibly cash in did. There were all sorts of books, for instance. Three in particular made an impression on me. One was a picture-book retelling the story of the movie. That story is not especially complicated: A farmboy intercepts a message from a princess imprisoned in a fortress far away. With the help of a wizard and a pirate, the farmboy rescues the princess and destroys the fortress. It is, unaided, about as childish a story as one could wish. Still this picture-book, directed at children by someone who must have had a rather low opinion of them, simplified the narrative even further. This had the no doubt intended effect of leaving lots of room for photographic stills from the film.

There was an incongruity in this book that I never forgot. It included a scene on Tatooine of Luke Skywalker visiting his friend Biggs Darklighter. This episode was supported by two photographs of Luke and Biggs together. Biggs looked older and more confident, with a dashing cape and moustache. I puzzled over this mystery quite a bit as a boy. I had no recollection of this character at all. I was certain I had not slept through this part of the movie; it was too early on. There was no Kenner figurine for Biggs, which counted against his existence but was not conclusive. One might think there had been some mistake but the photographs supported the book's account. I was a grown man before I got to the bottom of this, or nearly: Lucas had left these scenes on the cutting-room floor, yet somehow they made their way into this 1977 book to mystify me.

A much better book was an illustrated story called *Star Wars: the Mystery of the Rebellious Robot*. The main characters are Chewie, Han and Artoo, with appearances by Luke, Threepio, Leia and some mischievous Jawas. The illustrations are terrific. The inside of the Millennium Falcon is depicted in lustrous pastels, much more exciting than in the movie. Chewbacca is monstrous with dark eyes, a large mouth and maniacal hair. The prose is delightfully out of step with the undeviating, predictable, heavily trademarked lingo found without exception in later *Star Wars* material: Artoo and Threepio are "robots" not droids, Luke's X-wing fighter is his "plane", the Falcon is a "starship". The story itself revolves around the robots' fondness for oil baths, which the impish Jawas attempt to exploit for their own benefit. The whole notion of droids taking oil baths is very much one from the original *Star Wars* film and the earliest *Star Wars* era. There is nothing in the prequels to suggest that battle droids ever took them.

The third *Star Wars* book that has stayed with me over the years—quite literally—is a little blue hardback about the making of the film. In itself it is unremarkable. What is important about it is that I stole it. That is to say I withdrew it from the local public library and very consciously failed to return it. It is still in my basement today. This was the first of two incidents of childhood theft motivated by my lust for *Star Wars*.

The *Star Wars* soundtrack, which we had on LP, also served to keep the film ever-present in my mind. It came on two discs in a gatefold cover bearing the film's logo on the front, a frightening silhouette of Darth Vader's head against a field of stars on the back, and a collection of stills from the movie inside. The importance of John Williams' score to the success of *Star Wars* is impossible to prove but almost as hard to deny. Williams excites the audience from the opening frames—frames which are otherwise only words on a screen. For much of the rest of the film, Williams' score acts where the actors cannot, either because they are covered in metal or fibreglass or fur, or just because they cannot. The music is at points threatening, rollicking, touching and even conversational. *Star Wars* is unimaginable without it. Having said all that, I do not recall sitting around the house listening to this record as a five-year-old. But I probably did.

(Regrettably, we never owned a copy of Meco's disco remix, *Star Wars and Other Galactic Funk*. The single from that album stormed the charts in 1977, going platinum and holding the number one position on Billboard's Hot 100 for two weeks. Connoisseurs prefer the 12 inch, 15-minute-long version, the highlight of which is the Cantina-Band-inspired vibes solo at about 10 minutes in.)

Thus the story George Lucas told the world in *Star Wars* came to me only partly from his film. What I remembered of it made a profound impression, but I had only seen it once and had fallen asleep at its climax. The rest of the story—those parts I had slept through and those parts I had forgotten—reached me through other, disparate sources: the toys, books and music I have described, but also trading cards, television commercials, board games, and most importantly the recollections, embellishments and flat-out fantasies of other *Star-Wars*-mad children I knew.

The story that filtered through was, of course, a barely-disguised fairy tale. Even as a child I recognized, at once dimly and deeply, the archetypical nature of the characters and plot: the innocent abroad, the princess in distress, the virtuous pirate, the wise old man—all thrown together by circumstance or fate to overcome the forces of evil. But for me, the mythic aspect of *Star Wars* came not only from its plot and narrative form but also from the word-of-mouth means by which the story took root in my mind. Like other fairy tales, *Star Wars* was told and retold, with developments of its details and changes in emphasis in each retelling. Like other myths, *Star Wars* was part fact and part hearsay. In the earliest years of my infatuation with it, *Star Wars* was at once ubiquitous and elusive, and its elusiveness permitted—

even necessitated—imaginative retellings. The film was, in a word, evocative.

Star Wars would not have had this quality, however, had it not been such a good story to begin with. The characteristic that made *Star Wars* elusive to kindergarteners in the late 1970s was that you could only see it in cinemas and only when it was playing and only when your parents took you—but the same was true of every film of the day, yet only *Star Wars* metamorphosed from movie to myth. The difference lay in the strength of the story.

*

Were proof needed that *Star Wars* would be nothing if not for the strength of its story, that proof came on the evening of 17 November 1978 in the form of the *Star Wars Holiday Special.* The program was aired on the CBS television network in the United States and simultaneously in Canada on the CTV network. I saw it. I remember seeing it—sort of. I remember anticipating seeing it, possibly due to an ad in the newspaper. I remember the living room I saw it in: a plain rectangular room on the second floor of our Highland Place duplex with a picture window onto the cul-de-sac below and a faux-wood-panelled television in the corner. My recollections of the program itself are hazy, like a dream or an episode of déjà-vu. Unlike the real *Star Wars*, my memories of the *Holiday Special* are not reinforced by repeated viewings. It was shown once only, and will likely never been shown again. Of course the internet has now made it available for all to see as often as they like. Yet these internet versions betray their illicit, bootleg roots: the sound is poor, the video blurred or shaky. The reason is that George Lucas hates the *Star Wars Holiday Special*. He is said to have tried to buy all master copies of the program to destroy them, thus ensuring it was never seen again. What, one might ask, could be so distasteful to the man who wrote fart jokes into three different scenes of *The Phantom Menace*? The answer is complicated, but Art Carney, Bea Arthur, holo-porn and a singing Princess Leia figure prominently.

The plot, for want of a better word, concerns Chewbacca's efforts to return to his homeworld, Kashyyyk, in time to celebrate Life Day, a Wookie holiday for which no explanation is given. To make it home in time, Chewbacca and his pal Han Solo must overcome imperial forces who attack the Millennium Falcon en route and impose martial law at home. This might not be such a bad story if it were told with any conviction or interest. But the *Star Wars Holiday Special* is not about storytelling. It is a 1970s variety show with a *Star Wars* theme. Chewbacca, Han, Luke, Leia, Threepio and Artoo are hardly even in the show; they each make appearances from time to time, but most of the two-hour-long special is devoted to Chewbacca's family (wife Malla, son Lumpy and father Itchy—yes, Itchy), a "trader" named Saun Dann, the proprietor of the Mos Eisley cantina, Ackmena, musical guests Diahann Carroll and Jefferson Starship, and a dance outfit called the Wazzan Troupe.

The program starts inauspiciously with a ten-minute-long scene inside Chewbacca's tree-house in which no dialogue occurs save Wookie grunting. Chewbacca's forlorn wife, Malla, stares at a framed picture of Chewie and is comforted by Itchy, a murderous-looking ape with an old man's underbite and (we learn later) a taste for pornography. Itchy then turns his attention to young Lumpy, entertaining him with a hologram performance by dancing gymnasts dressed in skin-tight, insect-like green and red body suits. Some sport G-strings. This goes on for an eternity until Malla decides to call Luke on the videophone to find out where her husband is.

If the viewer has not noticed by now that the *Holiday Special* is a little strange, Luke's appearance removes all doubt. His hair is cut in a girlish bob, his eyelashes are bovine in length and he is wearing a quantity of make-up usually reserved for the dead. The explanation I once heard for this was that Mark Hamill had been in a serious motorcycle accident shortly before the filming. Whatever the reason, Luke looks awful, particularly when he grins creepily and says, "C'mon Malla, let's see a little smile".

Next we are introduced to the keeper of Trading Post Wookie Planet C, Saun Dann, played by Art Carney of *Honeymooners* fame. After failing to interest an imperial trooper in a "portable aquarium", Carney pops over to Malla's house—despite the imperial blockade of her planet—bearing Life Day presents for all. Carney's gift for Itchy is a hologram to be played in the family Mind Evaporator. This ominous-sounding device looks like a dentist's chair with a welder's helmet on top. By its name and appearance you would think it an instrument of torture, which it proves to be, for the viewing audience if not for Itchy. The decrepit Wookie climbs in and puts the mask on while Carney inserts his gift into the armrest. "Happy Life Day", says Carney, "and I do mean Happy Life Day". Itchy begins to masticate (yes, masticate) as swirling lights and ethereal music set the virtual stage for singer/actress Diahann Carroll, later known for her role as Dominique Deveraux in *Dynasty*. Carroll gets right to the point, thrilling Itchy with lines like, "Oh, oh...we are excited, aren't we?" and "I am your pleasure. Enjoy me". The camera cuts between Carroll, giggling and smiling, and Itchy, squirming and writhing. Carroll sings a song about infinitely extending this minute, repeating and repeating this minute, on and on and on and on. The lyrics could not be more appropriate—the song, like the entire *Holiday Special*, feels interminable.

While this Wookie sex fantasy is easily the strangest part of the program—and perhaps the strangest thing ever to be shown on network television—it is only one of many inexplicable episodes. There is the four-armed Chef Gormaanda (Harvey Korman, better known for his work on that other 1970s variety program, the *Carol Burnett Show*) guiding her audience unsuccessfully through a recipe for Bantha Surprise. There is Jefferson Starship playing a forgettable song with microphones and instruments glowing like violet lightsabers. There is the ten-minute cartoon in which Boba Fett makes his first appearance, searching for a magical talisman astride an enormous orange-pink dinosaur. There is Bea Arthur as Ackmena, the proprietor of a Tatooine cantina who persuades her patrons to abide by an imperial curfew by singing to them until they give in and clear out. There is Han Solo baring his soul to the Wookies with cringe-inducing expressions of familial affection. Finally there is Leia, taking it upon herself to address the Wookies about the significance of their own holiday in a vacuous sermon which concludes with her singing these words to the tune of the *Star Wars* theme:

We celebrate a day of peace / A day of harmony / A day of joy we can all share / Together joyously / A day that takes us through the darkness / A day that leads us into might / A day that makes us want to celebrate / The light / A day that brings the promise / That one day we'll be free / To live, to laugh, to dream, to grow, to trust, to love, to be!

Thankfully perhaps, most of what I have recounted here is not from memory. I vaguely recall the Wookie tree-house, Luke's strange appearance—like a damaged mannequin—and the Boba Fett cartoon, but I seem to have repressed the rest. Not until I was nearly thirty did I discover, thanks to the internet, that these foggy images in my mind were not childhood hallucinations but fragmentary recollections of a suppressed chapter in *Star Wars* history. Something I had read or heard about the forthcoming prequels taking place in part on the Wookie homeworld of Kashyyyk prompted my investigation. I recalled a portrayal of the planet in Marvel *Star Wars* number 91. But I also recalled seeing Wookies on television—with musical guests? A bit of digital digging turned up accounts of the *Holiday Special*, and even a few freeze frames from the program (but no video). I was amazed that I remembered the thing, however faintly, and more amazed that George Lucas had permitted it to be done.

*

All these things informed my earliest notions of what *Star Wars* was. But the movie was too inspiring and fleeting to confine me to any vision of it that was not my own. Building on what I remembered from the drive-in and what I gleaned from friends, toys, books, television and more, I imagined what *Star Wars* was and made it what I wanted it to be at any given moment.

Frequently this turned George Lucas's epic story into a protracted, repetitive and desolate tale of two adversaries stranded together on an island full of caves, plotting each other's demise in hand-to-hand combat. The cave-laden island was my favourite blanket, crumpled in a pile on my lap as I sat on the floor or in bed. The adversaries were Kenner action figures, one in each hand. Their identities depended on my mood, but I knew enough to tell the imperials from the rebels and generally respected this division of political opinion, which was the sole reason for their antagonism. Thus

Han Solo might find himself marooned with an imperial stormtrooper. Each would promptly resolve to annihilate the other. After an initial skirmish the figures would retreat to whatever cave they had each chosen and plot their next attempt. That event would ensue with little delay and again result in a draw and retreat. After another brief respite, the antagonists would meet again in the same violent and futile struggle, distinguished this time perhaps by some new move— pouncing on the other as he emerged unwarily from his cave, or pushing him over a cliff. I could amuse myself quietly for an hour or more this way. It is no wonder my parents were so willing to keep feeding my developing *Star Wars* habit.

A PIG WITH A STOMACH ACHE

In May 1980, the sequel to *Star Wars* was released. I was seven years old. It was the greatest thing that had ever happened. I saw *The Empire Strikes Back* for the first time in a movie theatre in the NorthPark shopping centre in Dallas, Texas during a visit with my grandparents. It was one of many such visits my mother, sister and I made in the early 1980s. Each trip saw my grandparents spoil my sister and me so that Dallas, my grandparents and *The Empire Strikes Back* are now nearly synonymous in my mind.

*

My grandparents' reaction to their only daughter becoming a hippy, marrying a Californian draft dodger and moving to Canada was what you might expect of mid-20th century middle-class Texans. When, before leaving for Canada, my mother brought my father home to meet her parents, my grandfather literally chased him out of the house. If the Vietnam War was not reason enough for my father to flee the country, my grandfather might have been.

Rollie Poston Bourland, known to most as Bob but to me as Clawpa, was a man of his place and time: a white Texan who picked cotton as a child, lived through the Depression and the war (he trained pilots but did not fight) and made his own way. He worked hard, earned a considerable amount of money, and rose to a prominent position in a national health insurance company. He had no sympathy for peaceniks or longhairs or Californians not named Nixon. If my mother was seeking to antagonize him, she could not have chosen a more effective instrument than my father.

My grandmother's frame of mind is less clear to me. She believed in God, I recall, but did not appear to have opinions about anything else. Perhaps she figured my grandfather had enough for the two of them. She had been attractive in her youth and still spent a lot of time "putting her face on" when I knew her, by which point she was in her early 60s. But she had a weakness bordering on addiction for Blue Bell Pecan Pralines 'n'

Cream ice cream, and as a result she developed a compact but very evident belly. As a child I marvelled at how it protruded from her. I do not remember my grandmother ever saying anything in particular about my father. I nevertheless had a distinct sense that he was not quite the son-in-law she had in mind.

My grandparents' misgivings about my father never expressed themselves in any sort of hostility or even coolness towards me or my sister. They were loving grandparents and always very generous with us. The frequent trips my mother, sister and I made to Dallas during my childhood—always wisely leaving my father behind—were as much shopping sprees as family visits. Every day was the same. For most of the morning my sister and I wandered around my grandparents' large air-conditioned one-storey house on East Lovers Lane, waiting hours, or so it seemed to us, for my grandmother to dress. My mother was faster, but not by much. When the four of us were finally ready to go we said goodbye to Clawpa—he always stayed home—and made our way down a small hallway off the kitchen to the dark two-car garage that adjoined the house. The humidity confronted us from the moment my mother opened the door. As my grandmother armed the alarm system—something I had never seen in Canada—my sister and I climbed in to the back seat of my grandmother's spotless Lincoln Town Car. It was yellow on the outside and yellow again inside. My grandmother took the driver's seat, started the car to get the air conditioning going, and gave me or my sister the garage door opener. We pressed it with delight and the door drew open, pouring Texas sunlight into the garage as we backed out into the alley. We hit the button again to close the door and were on our way.

Our destinations rarely changed. First we went to pick up my great-grandmother. Her name was Reva but I only ever knew her as Re Re (what my mother called her) and Mother (what my grandmother called her). Re Re was in her eighties but she was no little old lady. She was sturdy, deep-throated, tall for a woman born in 1899, and forceful. Picking Re Re up usually involved going inside her bungalow and waiting (again) while she prepared herself for the outing. My sister and I spent the time in the dark sitting-room banging on the electric organ she played hymns on, or running around her small back yard nearly bouncing off the thick Dallas grass. Once she was ready, we all squeezed back into the Town Car, turned on the air, and made for the NorthPark shopping centre.

NorthPark is no ordinary mall. I understand that better today than I did when I was seven, but even then I had a sense of it. It seemed endlessly large to me, bigger than Penticton. My mother explained that it was a sophisticated place, again in contrast to Penticton. It must be sophisticated, I reasoned, because it had a series of large indoor water fountains throughout the complex, and why would anyone build such things except for sophistication? The architecture of NorthPark was striking to me even as a boy: clean, simple, bright and unified despite the variety of shops it housed. The ceilings were high, the promenades spacious, and the centre's numerous lobbies and atriums displayed serious, large-scale modern art installations. NorthPark was full of shops, sounds and people I never saw back home. Every visit was stimulating.

But our next destination was my favourite: the Target department store in the Medallion Centre. The difference between the two shopping experiences could hardly have been greater. There was nothing chic or trendy about Target in the early 1980s. It was a discount department store with red-plastic shopping carts, clear-plastic clothes hangers, a greasy cafeteria and dozens of minimum-wage-earners staffing the aisles and checkout counters. But the most important difference between NorthPark and Target, as far as I was concerned, lay in its collection of *Star Wars* toys. You could find *Star Wars* toys in NorthPark's shops if you looked hard enough. But at Target you could hardly miss them. The store's toy section overflowed with them. Most impressive was the wall of Kenner action figures. It seemed eight feet high to me then and maybe it was—row after row, column after column of the objects of my seven-year-old desire. With the release of *Empire* Kenner's collection grew by some 30 figurines and they were all there at Target, though you might have to dig through a dozen imperial snowtroopers to find the ugnaught hidden at the back. Target's superabundance of *Star Wars* figures (and playsets, vehicles, T-shirts, lunchboxes, wristwatches, sleeping blankets...) made it easily my favourite place in Dallas, if not the world.

Target and NorthPark were our invariable destinations, but they were not the only ones. Dallas was full of shops of a nature and scale I had never seen in Penticton. The most striking was a travel- and safari-wear outfitter called Banana Republic. This store was full of khaki clothing, flight jackets, binoculars, compasses and other items that would not have looked out of place on the set of another hit movie of the day, *Raiders of the Lost Ark*. What made the Banana Republic shop memorable for me was not just its clothing but its adventure ambience, the crescendo of which was the full-sized bush plane that hung suspended from the ceiling. The place had an amusement park feel that NorthPark and Target could not match. I do not often go in to Banana Republic today, but when I do I am always disappointed. Other Dallas retail novelties included Pier 1 Imports, Goff's Hamburgers (the best I ever had, but then again I quit eating meat at age twelve) and a drive-through hot dog stand that was almost as exciting to my sister and me as the Target toy department.

These shopping trips would last all afternoon, leaving my sister and me quite exhausted by dinnertime. When we got home we hauled bag after bag of clothing and toys from the garage into the living room to show my grandfather. He looked on with some interest, never flinching no matter how much of his money we had spent. Later, however, in his bedroom which I always shared (my grandmother had her own at the other end of the house), he gently admonished me to save my money. At seven years old I did not have any money to save. Over thirty years later I still do not. But I have always remembered his advice and hope one day to take it.

*

To a true *Star Wars* fan, there are some things that go without saying. They are verities. To express them is unnecessary, even gauche. To dispute them would be a transparent admission of ignorance. Chief among these axioms is that *The Empire Strikes Back* is the best of the three (or, if you must, the six) *Star Wars* films. Please do not argue the point. You will only embarrass yourself.

Innocence pervades the original *Star Wars*. Luke, a farmboy living in ignorance of both his future and his past, finds himself suddenly thrown into alien worlds of wizardry, royalty, heroism and rebellion. At the film's climax, Luke trusts his instincts, and the mystical teachings of an unexpected mentor, to overcome the sprawling, mechanized, unfeeling Galactic Empire. The film's original viewers were also innocents, plunged into a fantasy world and a cinematographic experience like none they had ever seen.

The mood of *Empire* is distinctly different. If *Star Wars* is a story of innocence, *Empire* is one of experience, failure and betrayal. The contrast between the final scene of *Star Wars* and the opening scene of *Empire* sets the tone immediately: the celebrated heroes of the attack on the Death Star are now reduced to hiding from their enemies on a frozen, seemingly lifeless planet. Yet even there the Empire finds them. The appearance of a single probe droid is enough to provoke a complete evacuation of the rebel forces, but not before the Empire launches a massive ground assault on their base. The leader of this attack is Vader, no longer the junior man to Tarkin, now fully in command of the imperial forces from the bridge of a vessel that makes the gigantic Star Destroyer that swallowed Leia's ship in the opening scene of *Star Wars* look insignificant. Again in contrast to *Star Wars*, this time the rebels are routed. They are lucky to escape at all in the face of the giant imperial walkers bestriding Hoth's frozen surface and the fearsome imperial fleet waiting in its orbit. The mood of *Empire* does not let up. Though lightened throughout by humour and even a touch of romance, these respites only accentuate the film's pervasive darkness. Han and Chewbacca, charged once again with saving Leia, repeatedly fail to escape their pursuers, let down superficially by their ship but really by themselves. Luke's failures are more pronounced. Travelling to Dagobah to be trained by a Jedi master, Luke does not even know Yoda when he sees him. The ancient teacher initially refuses to take him on, asking Obi-Wan pointedly, "Will he finish what he begins?" The answer proves to be No. After repeated failures and disappointments, Luke abandons his training to save his friends—which he does not. Han is betrayed, tortured, frozen in carbonite and delivered to a bounty hunter. Leia, Chewbacca and Threepio escape (the latter carried in pieces on Chewbacca's back) but not due to Luke's intervention. On the contrary, it is Leia who saves Luke after a disastrous confrontation with Vader. This duel, the film's startling climax, leaves Luke disfigured for a second time: he was mauled by an abominable snowman earlier in the film and now he loses his right hand. Worse is the trauma of Vader's horrible revelation. Ben had lied: Vader is not Luke's father's murderer but Luke's murderous father.

The contrast between *Star Wars* and *Empire* reached also to the films' audiences. The first viewers of *Star Wars* were thrilled in part because their expectations were so low. No one had ever made a film like *Star Wars* before, such that every novelty was refreshing, every innovation an improvement on what had come before. For *Empire* the situation was almost the opposite. Never had expectations for a film been so high. There seemed nowhere to go but down. The film's director, Irvin Kershner, originally rejected the offer to direct the *Star Wars* sequel for that very reason—how could it do anything but disappoint? His agent persuaded him to reconsider. Kershner's job then became to make a sequel that would at least live up to the most popular movie of all time. He surpassed it.

It was during one of our Dallas shopping trips that I first saw *Empire*. We caught the matinee at the NorthPark cinema. I remember emerging from the theatre into a bright, clear, stifling Texas afternoon reeling with excitement over what I had just seen. It must have been in late June or early July 1980, shortly after the school year had ended and a month or so after *Empire* had been released. It was not until I was well in to writing this book that I recalled that my grandmother had come with my mother, my sister and me to see the film. It amazes me now to think of that. She was not, to my knowledge, even an occasional filmgoer, and science fiction (as she would have considered it) was as remote and uninteresting to her as Hegelian dialectic. She had almost certainly not seen *Star Wars*, and *Empire* was hardly a stand-alone film: Lucas and company clearly felt entitled—with justification—to assume that every viewer of the sequel had seen the precursor at least once. So for my grandmother to come see *The Empire Strikes Back* at the NorthPark matinee must have been an act of pure indulgence of her grandchildren.

The film was exciting and mysterious from the moment the subtitle "Episode V: THE EMPIRE STRIKES BACK" floated across the screen. I could not recall any such subtitle to *Star Wars*, and in fact there had been none; Lucas dubbed this film Episode V and rechristened his previous work "Episode IV: A New Hope" in re-releases. The immediate effect of this storytelling device was to make me want to see Episodes I, II and III—films that had not yet been made, or even written. I carried this desire with me for nineteen years, when it was pitilessly driven out of me in the first three minutes of *The Phantom Menace*. For the moment, however, I was fascinated by the implications of this simple phrase, "Episode V", and transfixed by the words that followed it into space, beginning aptly with "It is a dark time for the Rebellion…". For the next two hours I was completely engrossed by *Empire*'s contrasts: gravity and levity, friendship and betrayal, mystery and revelation, all at relentless pace yet intelligible even to a seven-year-old. I left the cinema dizzy with excitement. How soon could I see it again? And how soon could I see the sequel?

The only reaction I remember my grandmother having to *Empire* was to ask, with real puzzlement, "Who was that little green man?" I had the same question. Yoda was one of the mysteries that made *Empire* so intriguing. Who was he? The Jedi master who instructed him, Ben had said. But there was clearly much more to Yoda than that. Besides, Ben said in *Star Wars* that the Jedi were gone. Tarkin had said the same, telling Vader, "The Jedi are extinct, their fire has gone out of the universe". Yet here was Yoda, a sort of lizard man living alone in a swamp, and a Jedi master. What was the explanation? What was the story? And what, for that matter, was Yoda? I later learned, probably on the back of a trading card, that he was nine hundred years old. I took this to mean he was a nine-hundred-year old man, shrunken and discoloured with extreme age. How he had developed cloven feet, long ears and three-digit hands was hard to understand, but who knew what might happen to a person after nine centuries? But maybe he was not a man at all—nothing was explained. We were left to guess. My grandmother's speculation was as valid as anyone's. "He looked to me", she said, "like a pig with a stomach ache".

My mother's reaction to *Empire* also stayed with me. Driving to our next destination after seeing the film, she gave voice to a feeling I had never heard her express. Very mildly, completely inoffensively to anyone who was not her seven-year-old son, she said something to the effect that Harrison Ford was a very attractive man. I was bewildered. I lacked not only the vocabulary but the sensibility to explain, or even understand, my reaction. It was not that my mother was not supposed to take notice of men who were not my father. She was not supposed to take notice of men at all. This was not jealousy on my part. It was not protectiveness. It was stark fact: mothers, fathers, teachers, human beings in general were neuters. Of course I had heard, and even told, jokes about boys and girls on the playground. And there was that time when the girl from across the street came to play in our basement. But the usual thing was that boys and girls, men and women paid no attention to each other. There was little in *Star Wars* to dissuade me of any of this. But *Empire* was different. Of course when Leia kissed Luke, it was a joke. A little more courageous than the playground jokes I knew, but still a joke. She did it to make Han mad. But why did it make Han mad? And later, when Han kissed Leia on board the Millennium Falcon, it was not quite as clearly a joke. Threepio interrupted them, and that was funny, but the kissing part seemed not to be a joke at all. It was hard to say; there were a lot of jokes in *The Empire Strikes Back*. But there was something else, too. My mother called it romance. It was something I would not learn anything more about from George Lucas.

*

Seven year olds were not the only ones happy to finally see the *Star Wars* sequel hit the theatres. Cincinnati's luckiest toy company was about to strike it rich again, and this time it knew it.

Kenner began whetting children's appetites for new *Empire* action figures in 1979 with a free Boba Fett promotion: just mail four *Star Wars* action figure proof-of-purchase seals to Boba Fett Offer, One Industrial

Drive, Box 2520, Maple Plain, MN 55348 and Kenner will send you a free Boba Fett with Rocket Firing Back Pack. Or so they said. In fact Kenner ended up sending out a Boba Fett without the spring-loaded, rocket-firing backpack. Instead the figure came with an apology letter from Kenner explaining that the figure's most exciting feature had been removed for safety reasons. Never mind—Boba Fett was still a great figure, and there were more to come.

Kenner's initial *Empire Strikes Back* range consisted of 22 figures, roughly doubling the total number of *Star Wars* action figures on the market. The best, in my mind, were those to do with the ice planet Hoth. Maybe it was a Canadian thing, but I loved the "Hoth Battle Gear" versions of Han Solo, Luke Skywalker and Imperial Stormtrooper, all kitted out in winter coats, boots and gloves. Even Princess Leia Organa (described as wearing a "Hoth Outfit" rather than battle gear) was well done. Other admirable additions were Luke Skywalker (Bespin Fatigues) with his much-improved (but still yellow) lightsaber, Imperial Commander (the closest Kenner ever came to a proper Tarkin figure), and Dengar, a character—if you can call him that—who appears on screen for a matter of seconds but whom Kenner nevertheless rendered beautifully in 3¾ inch form. The level of detail in these figures was easily superior to that of most of the original *Star Wars* offerings.

But there were nevertheless some curiosities, and some duds, in Kenner's *Empire* range. Yoda, for instance, was quite a good figure in many ways. But why was he wearing an orange snake around his neck? And why did the Bespin Security Guard figure come in two versions, one a fat-headed white man with a moustache (even though the photo on the card clearly showed him with a full beard) and the other a very dark-skinned black man? I somehow ended up with both figures; commendably uninterested in their racial differences, I ignored them both equally. In a universe of Jedi knights, stormtroopers, droids and bounty hunters, who has time to waste on a mere security guard? Bespin spawned as many bad Kenner figures as Hoth spawned good ones. Lando Calrissian was the most disappointing—Kenner attempted ham-fistedly to capture Calrissian's charisma with a toothy grin and gleaming white eyes. The effect was ridiculous, especially when contrasted with the blank or even sullen expressions on the faces of most of Kenner's other hero figurines. A variation of the Lando figure with brown instead of white for the eyes and mouth was an improvement, but both versions sported an unflattering baby blue tunic and a cheap plastic cape with armholes like those found, with equally unsatisfying effect, on the Darth Vader and Obi-Wan Kenobi figurines. Cloud Car Pilot and Ugnaught were two more Bespin figures of little interest, despite their unusual accessories: a comlink for the former and a funny little white briefcase for the latter.

Kenner's *Empire Strikes Back* line was, of course, not limited to action figures. The company also created new playsets and vehicles drawn from the film. Again the best of these came from the Hoth battle sequences. The stand-out for me was the Imperial Attack Base. Strictly this belonged to my sister, but by this point she was beginning to lose interest in *Star Wars* toys and it would not be long now before she gave her entire collection to me in an exchange rivalling the Dutch purchase of Manhattan in exploitative one-sidedness. Even before this momentous trade, the Imperial Attack Base playset was effectively mine. The toy was a piece of white plastic, about the size of a small board game, sculpted to look like an iceberg or snow fort with room inside for three or four figurines to move around. To this simple set-up was added a rotating black laser cannon, a military-grey pergola dubbed a command post, a snow stairway leading to an ice bridge, and a hidden land mine which, when triggered, sent the figure standing upon it flying into the air. Both the ice bridge and the command post had secret triggers to collapse them at opportune moments. In short, this playset packed hours of imaginative (if violent) play into quite a small space. It was a winner by any reasonable standard. Its superiority was especially obvious when measured against previous Kenner playsets, many of which consisted of little more than a coloured plastic base with a few footpegs and a cardboard backdrop. Where Kenner really outdid itself, however, was with the AT-AT (All Terrain Armoured Transport). I did not have one. The boy who lived across the street did.

*

Nathan Barlow became my best friend soon after we moved to Penticton. He was one year younger than me, all smiles and freckles, and, by 1980, easily the funniest person I had ever known. He seemed always to be saying amusing, even uproarious things, none of which I can now recall. During sleepovers at our house, Nathan frequently made me laugh so convulsively that I began to heave, often actually throwing up from too much laughter. If my sister was with us (as she usually was) the sight and smell of my vomiting would provoke her to throw up, too. My mother was almost as fond of Nathan as I was, but she did not much care for cleaning up our puke every time he spent the night. After several instances of hilarity-induced vomiting, mum told Nathan he was not allowed to spend the night any more. In any case I preferred going to his house where we could play with his AT-AT.

Kenner's AT-AT was a giant toy—about a foot and a half high and nearly two feet long. Unlike other Kenner versions of large vehicles or settings, which made no attempt to replicate the original's dimensions or scale (for example, Death Star Space Station and Land of the Jawas), the AT-AT, while certainly not to scale, successfully approximated the exhilarating proportions of *Empire*'s Hoth battle scenes. What other Kenner toy could accommodate ten figurines in the cargo bay and two more in the cockpit? Its size alone made the AT-AT exciting. But the AT-AT was also a very decent likeness of *Empire*'s imperial walkers in other respects: form, colour, details. Faithfulness to the films was a hallmark of all Kenner's best work, and the AT-AT had it.

Like just about every other boy I knew, Nathan shared my ardour for *Star Wars*, which expressed itself chiefly in a large collection of Kenner toys. Maybe because he was a year younger than me, or maybe because his parents' fortunes were suddenly (and temporarily) rising at the time, Nathan's collection consisted mostly of *Empire* tie-ins: the AT-AT, a Rebel Armoured Snowspeeder with its pulsating yellow laser lights and removable harpoon gun, a Tauntaun with the wonderfully named "Open Belly Rescue Feature", an R2-D2 with retractable periscope, and just about every other action figure from the second film. Conversely, my collection featured more original *Star Wars* items: the Millennium Falcon, a TIE Fighter, Luke's landspeeder, a Dewback. Between us we had a fair portion of Kenner's entire production by 1981. But we both wanted more.

Nathan's mother received the Sears *Wish Book* catalogue in the mail every autumn. The *Wish Book* was a thick, glossy, newsprint-format catalogue for Christmas shopping. Almost every one of its 400-plus pages was crammed full of colour photographs displaying the thousands of items available from Sears on mail order: clothing, appliances, furniture, electronics, linens, kitchenware, garden tools, pool tables, cosmetics, typewriters, hockey gear, bicycles and of course toys. The toy section devoted one or two full pages to *Star Wars*, sometimes displaying Kenner's figures and other offerings in dioramas. Nathan and I studied these pages like scholars when the catalogue first arrived, starting with the toy section but later scouring the rest of the catalogue, too, as *Star Wars* products were increasingly finding their way into other sections: children's clothing, bedding, even costume jewellery. (My sister once owned a gold-coloured C-3PO pendant.) Anything new excited our greatest attention, but old items were also of interest if we did not yet have them. Some weeks later, when the novelty of the catalogue had worn off, we would still come back to it from time to time, just to admire its arrangements of figurines and vehicles—or perhaps to stare, with an interest I still found inexplicable, at photographs elsewhere in the catalogue of women modelling modest lingerie.

Even better than the Sears catalogues were Kenner's own promotional pamphlets. These were glossy rectangular booklets, roughly the dimensions of a postcard, inserted by Kenner into the packaging of its larger toys. Each of the dozen or so pages of these mini catalogues displayed action figures, vehicles, playsets and various oddball items like Switcheroos (*Star-Wars*-themed faceplates for light switches) and Play-Doh Action Play Sets, all in full colour photos displayed on black pages with white text. At seven years old, there was little I wanted out of life that was not contained within the pages of one of these booklets.

Nathan was my best friend but also the victim of my second *Star-Wars*-motivated crime. IG-88 was a tall, especially mechanical-looking droid who stood in line with Boba Fett, Bossk and Dengar in the brief scene in *Empire* when Vader instructs the bounty hunters he has recruited to find Luke Skywalker. IG-88 made no other appearance in the film, or any of the films. (Predictably, the droid has been given a long and convoluted backstory in the so-called Expanded Universe.) IG-88 had no lines to speak and no part to play in the film other than standing to attention in one brief scene. Nevertheless Kenner made a figure out of the thing, and I had it. But somehow I lost its gun. This was highly unusual for me. I was meticulous about knowing which weapon belonged to which figurine and ensuring that none got lost or even misfiled in some other figure's slot in my Kenner carrying cases. IG-88's gun was a slight variation on the gun found on Kenner's snowtrooper figures: a long blaster rifle, but bearing one grip instead of two. No other Kenner figure came with this distinctive weapon. So I was very disappointed to have lost it—so much so that I stole Nathan's right from under his nose while we played together one day. He detected the theft immediately and rightly accused me. I denied everything and told him he must have lost his IG-88 rifle because this one was mine. He did not believe me, but somehow I must have persuaded him because when I left his house that day I had the weapon with me. I still have it today, in my basement with the rest of my collection. I felt guilty over what I had done almost immediately, but I was too embarrassed to admit my dishonesty, apologize and return the pilfered accessory. Having gone this far down the path of petty criminality, it was hard to turn back, much easier to pretend that I had never turned down it at all. I expected to one day forget my lie, or conveniently come to believe it. I never did.

Despite this shabby episode, Nathan was undoubtedly my best friend. I hardly remember having any others at the time. *Star Wars* and vomit were not all we had in common. We walked to school together, played street hockey on weekends and palled around in the summers and holidays. We once fell out of a tree together. He landed on a rock and smashed his head. I then landed on him and smashed it again. The tree was a pine or fir beside Nathan's duplex, across the street from our own duplex. As I fell I saw my mother, standing at our living room's picture window, watching with horror as we tumbled out of the platform Nathan's brothers had built in the tree.

Clearer still is my recollection of Nathan's departure from Penticton. His father had got a new job in Flin Flon, Manitoba, a mining town on the Saskatchewan border that made Penticton look like Vienna. The news that Nathan was moving away was a shock to me. I had had the good fortune of never suffering an emotional loss before—none of my relatives had died, none of my pets had run away, and my parents were still married. As the day of Nathan's departure approached, I experienced for the first time the sensation of dread. Finally one summer evening it was time for Nathan and his family to go. The movers had taken their things away already. As Nathan's parents finished packing up their Chevy Suburban for the first leg of the 2,000 kilometre drive, friends and neighbours gathered to see the family off. One of Nathan's uncles tried to teach me how to catch a football but I was not concentrating. Nathan was as cheerful as ever, smiling and looking forward to the trip. As the day faded, Nathan's dad pulled the truck out of the driveway and into the cul-de-sac. We all said our final goodbyes in the blue-violet light. Nathan and his brothers climbed into the back seat of the truck and waved to us through the rear window as they drove away. My sister and I waved back, and I ran a little ways after the truck. Nathan was still smiling, but I had a lump in my throat.

*

From the beginning of my *Star Wars* obsession, my sister had joined in. This was partly out of ardour for *Star Wars* and partly the natural behaviour of a younger sister towards her big brother; she was always joining in, as reliably as Momma Cat followed us around the cul-de-sac. Sissy Bobo, as I still call her, played *Star Wars* with me but also Lego, hide-and-seek, ball hockey, grasshopper-catching and just about everything else. But by the time *Empire* came out, Sissy (now five) was developing her own interests, especially books and horses. Her interest in *Star Wars* remained, but waned. It may be that Kenner's tendency to market its products to boys, especially in television commercials, was giving her the impression that this was not a suitable enthusiasm for a girl. Or perhaps she just got a little bored with what was, after all, a fairly repetitive pastime.

What became my *Star Wars* toy collection was based in large part on toys given to my sister, almost always from my grandparents at Christmas or during our visits to Dallas. After some squabbling about which action figures belonged to whom, my mother began marking those belonging to my sister with a dab of pink nail polish applied to the sole of the figure's foot. About half of the figures now stored in my basement, and dating from the original film, are marked in this way. Some of my *Empire*-era figurines are also so marked. My mother did not mark the vehicles or playsets, but many of these were once my sister's, too. A year or two after *Empire* came out, my sister offered to give me her entire collection. All she asked in return was that I let her play with me sometimes. She has since told me that I had become impatient with playing *Star Wars* with her, and that by offering me her entire collection—roughly as large as my own at that point—she sought to bargain her way back into my playtime. She wanted to spend more time with her older brother, and she knew that *Star Wars* was the way to his heart. I readily accepted this hugely one-sided deal and moved the entire mass of figurines, vehicles and playsets into my room.

In later years the inequity of this bargain grew all-the-more obvious. My sister cunningly reminded me of it at strategically advantageous moments. For the rest of our childhoods, and even beyond, at any time Sissy sought some concession or favour from me she would invoke this monumental gift and invite me to redress the great imbalance that had hung over our relationship from that day forward by letting her come along, sharing my ice cream sandwich with her, helping with her chores, lending her my stereo, driving her to her friend's house, not telling mum, and so on. Valuing these toys as highly as I did, this technique was usually effective on me. When, years later, my sister married, her gift of *Star Wars* toys and the years of emotional blackmail that had come with it figured prominently in my Toast to the Bride.

[JEDI]
DOWN WITH THE SHIP

There has never been a more anticipated film than *Return of the Jedi*. For three years after the release of *The Empire Strikes Back*, audiences around the world had to wait to learn the fate of Han Solo, to know what would come of Darth Vader's shocking revelation, and to see if the Rebellion would finally overcome the Empire. For that part of the world's film-going population over the age of ten, this wait was probably not terribly onerous. For me and many of my boyhood friends, it was agonizing. *The Empire Strikes Back* was a cliff I hung from for three years. The same was not true in the period between *Star Wars* and *Empire*. *Star Wars* was not a cliff-hanger and I was not immediately aware of an impending sequel. In any case I was too young to sustain a long anticipation of anything. Between *Empire* and *Jedi*, however, I was acutely aware of what the future would bring. The way *Empire* ended was proof enough that a sequel was coming. Television, newspapers and magazines—all of which I began to understand and pay attention to at this time—provided occasional confirmation of the obvious, sometimes offering tantalizing hints of what the sequel had in store. But it was years away. In the meantime, this fantasy world that had become my obsession was placed in suspended animation, like Han Solo frozen in carbonite.

Three years is a long time to wait for anything. All the more so for a seven year old for whom three years is almost half a life. As obsessed as I was, I could not fill three years' worth of a first-world child's spare time with nothing but *Star Wars*. I had to find other things to do with myself. I briefly played hockey, baseball and soccer but was no good at any of them and did not keep them up. I remained interested in hockey, however. Penticton was a hockey-crazed town with a glorious history. The 1954 Allan Cup champions, the Penticton Vees, represented Canada in the 1955 world championship, defeating the Soviet Union 5-0 in the final game of the tournament. Penticton had a strong team again in the 1980s, the Penticton Knights. My family billeted one of the team's sixteen-year-old players, Morey Gare (younger brother to Danny, the well-known Buffalo

Sabre). We often went to the games at Memorial Arena, a beautiful old rink that also serves as a shrine to the Vees and other Penticton teams of old. During intermissions I walked around the rink studying the dozens of old photographs, trophies and news clippings proudly displayed on the arena's walls. If I was not at the game I listened to the play-by-play on the local AM radio station, the risibly-named CKOK. My father and I also watched the Vancouver Canucks on television as they made their surprise run in the 1982 Stanley Cup playoffs, winning the Campbell Conference championship but losing the Cup final four games to none to the extraordinary New York Islanders.

Around this time my parents bought me a BMX-style bike, the first real bike I ever had. Shortly after Nathan left town we moved a few blocks away, from Highland Place to Allison Street (another duplex). Riding for hours in the evenings and weekends, I minutely explored the new neighbourhood. Though I was never more than eight blocks from home, I took an exhilarating sense of freedom from these excursions. On summer evenings when school was out I climbed the hill up Allison Street to Lawrence Avenue and beyond to Jodi Little's house, in the hope of catching a sight of her. On the way I thought of what to say if I did happen to find her—how to make it seem like a fortunate accident rather than the half-understood pre-pubescent urge that it was. But on the rare occasions when I did find her, on her front lawn or walking with her parents, I got nervous, made a mess of it and quickly headed home in a self-inflicted rout.

Rudimentary home computing was beginning at this time. My great-uncle Kenney (Clawpa's younger brother) and his wife Evelyn gave my sister and me an Atari 2600. Kenney and Evelyn were excessively generous with us. But they never gave me *Star Wars* presents, and I was always initially disappointed with their gifts for that reason. Later my paternal grandmother, whom I barely knew, gave us a Texas Instruments TI-99/4A computer. I hooked it up to our television (these first computers never came with monitors) and began to teach myself BASIC. I showed some talent for it, and I enjoyed it. But I did not keep it up.

There was ample time between 1980 and 1983 for me to develop other interests. There was time enough even to lose interest in *Star Wars* altogether, to move on to something new. I never did. I had other pastimes, other enthusiasms, but nothing supplanted, or even rivalled, *Star Wars*. Everything gave way to it.

*

By late 1982 the marketing push for the next film was under way—before its title had been finally decided upon. Twentieth Century Fox famously released a teaser poster for "Revenge of the Jedi" featuring Luke and Vader duelling against a red and black background of Vader's masked head. I have a memory of seeing this poster on display outside the Pen-Mar cinema, but I may be mistaken as the poster was apparently rare. Another part of the 1982 marketing hype was Kenner's latest mail-in offer, a free Admiral Ackbar figure from "Star Wars: Revenge of the Jedi". I never sent away for it, but the promotion had the desired effect of intriguing me even further about the upcoming film.

It was probably not a coincidence that 1982 was also the year *Star Wars* first appeared on VHS, pay-per-view and cable television. Pay television began in Canada in early 1983 with the debut of a national service called First Choice (later First Choice Superchannel). The service was free for a fourteen-day preview period during which *Star Wars* was shown repeatedly. After that the signal was scrambled and would-be viewers were invited to subscribe. We did not do so. I doubt we could have afforded it. In any case there was no need as my father had figured out a way to pick up the signal using rabbit ears and tin foil, and neither he nor my mother had any compunction about doing so. The picture was not always clear, and we often had to get off the couch and play with the antenna to improve the reception. I sometimes stood for half an hour holding the rabbit ears at just the right angle to keep the picture steady while I watched a program from less than a foot away. But it mostly worked. Suddenly there was a way for me to see *Star Wars*, and later *Empire*, repeatedly.

The First Choice viewing guide came out once a month in magazine format on glossy newsprint. Despite our illicit access to the service, we always seemed to have a copy of the viewing guide. Every month, when the new guide appeared, I scoured the listings for showtimes. First Choice was not very obliging; it would show *Star Wars* at 11 am on a Tuesday, while I was at school, or at 9 pm on a weeknight, when I was supposed to be in bed. More than once I was driven to faking illness to catch the movie the only time it was showing that week, or even that month. Having identified the showtime days in advance, I carefully laid the foundations of my alibi. A cough two or three days before, well within earshot of my mother. A stomach ache after dinner the night before. Then, that morning, listlessness in bed. My mother, who never suspected me of any dishonesty, fell for the routine easily. If I played it especially well, I need not even tell her I was sick. She made the decision for me: I was staying home from school today. Then, come 11 am, snug in blankets and propped up with pillows in the living room, perhaps with a bowl of tomato soup in my hands, First Choice announced its "Feature Presentation". The screen fell black, and then the famous words appeared: A long time ago in a galaxy far, far away... Look mum, *Star Wars* is on!

*

Star Wars, and popular movies in general, are routinely described as a form of escapism. That concept has little application to a four-year-old boy, however. In early childhood, fantasy and reality are places on the same continuum. Learning to distinguish between the two is one of the things we mean by growing up. Even as the distinction becomes apparent, however, a happy child does not need to escape from reality. Fantasy is a pleasure, not a refuge. Neither *Star Wars* nor *Empire* was escapism for me. But in the years between *Empire* and *Jedi*, I did have something to escape from. My parents' fortunes, and their marriage, were increasingly strained.

My father changed jobs nearly as often as my mother changed religions. He was a bank teller, a debt collector, a car salesman, an event photographer, an ice cream man, a car salesman again (now at a different dealership), a real estate agent, and more. Some of the jobs my father switched in and out of were joint efforts between my mother and father to start their own business, a would-be solution to their financial problems which allowed my mother to express her creativity while also accommodating my father's constitutional inability to be anyone's employee. My mother increasingly felt that if my sister and I were to have any stability and security in our lives, she was going to have to provide it herself. She would have to become the income-earner. From this realization it was only a short step to divorce, a prospect she began to look forward to as eagerly as I awaited *Return of the Jedi*. Arguments between my parents increased in frequency and unpleasantness, though thankfully without ever being drunken or violent. While I did not appreciate it at the time, the frequent trips my mother, sister and I made to Dallas were not only to visit my grandparents but to give my mother some respite from her failing marriage.

One consequence of my parents' financial troubles in the early 1980s was that we moved house every year or so. The worst place we lived, from an aesthetic and perhaps even a hygienic perspective, was the former front office of a twenty-room, 1950s-era motel. The old motel rooms, situated behind our unit in an L-shape with parking spots in front of each door, were rented out to people in even worse straits than us. My sister and I were forbidden to go back there, and we did not want to. There were no children there (mercifully), only oddballs, hard luck cases and rough characters—men who did not wear as many clothes as the weather demanded, and women who did not mind. All this was directly behind us, connected to our home by walls and ceiling. The sensation I most associate with living there was a determination to keep looking forward, not to turn around, not to look back.

The motel-house had one thing going for it, namely that it was directly across the street from Penticton's greatest attraction: the long, golden-sanded beaches of Okanagan Lake. For all its drawbacks, living in the motel-house was like being on an extended vacation— sun, sand, water and hundreds of generally happy people just outside our door for about four months of the year. The view from the beach was thrilling. Due north was the enormous grey-blue lake merging with the green-blue hills on a far away, sky-blue horizon broken every ten minutes or so by the sight of a delighted holidaymaker floating through the air supported by a multi-coloured parasail on one end and a speedboat on the other. To the west, parked at the lakeshore no more than a one-minute walk from our front door, were the partly-restored remnants of the S.S. Sicamous, a 200-foot-long, steel-hulled, steam-powered, white-painted sternwheeler that ferried passengers up and down the lake from 1914 until the mid-1930s. My sister and I never quite knew what to make of it, but it was picturesque and mysterious, and added to the holiday-carnival unreality of living there. Far to the east but unmistakably visible was Munson Mountain, a gentle, half-desert hill like all the others that surrounded us, except that on this one the proud citizens of Penticton had, at some distant point in the town's past, painstakingly laid out thousands of white pebbles in gigantic letters to spell PENTICTON on its side—as if to proclaim, to everyone splashing in the water and sunning themselves on the beach miles below, that they were doing precisely the things for which this place was intended. All this was wonderful. Just don't look back.

The principal reason for moving to the motel-house was that it was cheap. But it was also close to the site of my parents' new business: a former garage in a semi-industrial part of town which my mother had convincingly renovated into a fitness studio. How my parents ever hit upon a fitness studio I do not know.

There was a craze at the time, led by Jane Fonda's workout books and videos. But my parents were not sporty. They were not even particularly healthy. My mother had quit smoking but my father had not, and while my mother was naturally small and slender she had no strength or definition to speak of. My father was positively overweight for much of my early childhood, and though he had slimmed down considerably by the early 1980s he was far from fit. And yet their fitness studio in a disused garage in the wrong part of town was a moderate success.

The entrance was completely unremarkable—a dingy two-storey beige commercial building with no signage or visual appeal, situated immediately next to a 7-Eleven and across the street from a Jeep dealership. The front door opened onto a dark corridor with one or two cheap wooden doors on either side giving access to small, dull offices—the kind an aspiring member of Parliament would rent for a month then abandon when his campaign failed. At the end of the corridor was the entrance to the fitness studio, again concealed behind an ugly door. But having made your way through the dreariness, the studio was a splendour. Unlike the rest of the building, the space was not divided into two storeys. Instead its ceiling was twenty feet high, a design that was probably intended to accommodate whatever light industry the building was originally designed for. The dimensions were simple: the space was an enormous empty box. There was no exercise equipment—no dumbbells, no Nautilus machines, no benches. Only a wide, empty dance floor with a wall of nine-feet-high mirrors on the west side. There were no windows, but the rear wall consisted of a large garage door letting onto the back alley. When opened, southern light would stream through, illuminating the floor, the mirrors and the disco ball my mother had hung from the ceiling. Between the entrance and the dance floor was a lounge of low benches decorated with colourful throw pillows and a steep, floating staircase leading to a small, tree-fort-like office tucked into the northeast corner of the studio. Looking out the glassless window my sister and I could watch the aerobics, kung fu and even breakdance classes below. If *Star Wars* is forever associated in my mind with Highland Place, and *The Empire Strikes Back* with Dallas, Texas, then the Base (as my mother named this new venture) is the place I most connect to *Return of the Jedi*.

*

The film I had been waiting three years to see was finally released on 25 May 1983. I watched Leonard

Maltin's enthusiastic review of it on *Entertainment Tonight* shortly before opening night. Leonard Maltin was all I knew about film criticism in 1983, and his stamp of approval was, in my mind, decisive: the new *Star Wars* film was great. Nine out of ten, if I remember correctly.

I saw *Return of the Jedi* at the Pen-Mar cinema either on opening night or shortly thereafter. The Pen-Mar was Penticton's only movie theatre since the drive-in had shut down. (The Pen was for Penticton and the Mar was for Martin Street, or so I assume.) There was a murmur of anticipation as we queued for tickets and milled about the Pen-Mar's small concession area, full as fire department regulations would allow, waiting for the doors to open. There were only two screens in the complex, and both were showing *Jedi*. While I remember these moments before seeing the film quite well, I draw a blank on most everything else. I cannot remember who I saw the film with. I cannot remember any immediate reactions I had to it. I loved *Return of the Jedi* and felt none of the ambivalence about it that I heard other *Star Wars* fans express many years later. Yet there may be something telling in the fact that my initial viewing of the film was my least memorable film-going experience of the three. But I say that with nearly thirty years of hindsight; though I do not specifically recall leaving the theatre raving about the best movie I had ever seen, I'm sure I did.

The marketing and merchandising of *Jedi* found an easy mark in me, as usual. By now I had small amounts of my own money—an allowance of $1 a week contributed by my grandparents and earnings from a paper route—to spend on *Jedi* toys and tie-ins. Action figures remained the focus of my attention. I collected nearly all the *Jedi* figures between 1983 and 1985, including the entirely pointless ones made for the sole purpose of swindling little *Star Wars* addicts like me out of their money three dollars at a time. I mean figures like Prune Face and Klaatu In Skiff Guard Outfit (as opposed to ordinary Klaatu—Kenner actually made two figures for a 'character' that had no dialogue in the film at all, and I was dumb enough to buy them both). On the whole, however, the quality of the Kenner *Jedi* figures was superior to anything the company had done before. Bib Fortuna, Lando Calrissian (Skiff Guard Disguise), Luke Skywalker (Jedi Knight Outfit) and Princess Leia Organa (In Combat Poncho) were especially well done. But Kenner showed little discretion in selecting characters from the film to make into figures; just about every character in *Jedi*, however minor, was given its toy counterpart. (One exception comes to mind—Mon Mothma. Why she was left out when General Nadine went in is hard to understand.)

I bought many of my *Return of the Jedi* action figures at the Bay, a department store chain that had a location directly across the street from the Pen-Mar. The Bay is a sort of Canadian institution. It was founded in 1670, under the magnificent name "The Governor and Company of Adventurers of England trading into Hudson's Bay", as a means of exploiting the fur trade and expanding British possessions in North America. Well into the twentieth century, Hudson Bay Company trading posts and stores were the only commercial outlets to be found in many Canadian towns. Despite this swashbuckling history, by 1983 the Bay was mostly just a department store, and a rather staid one at that. But they sold *Star Wars* toys, and every time my mother brought me shopping there I would climb the stairs to the third floor toy department in search of new releases.

In contrast to the permanence and mild dreariness of the Bay was the opening, at about this time, of Penticton's first 7-Eleven convenience store. The arrival of a new American franchise causes a certain excitement in a small Canadian town even now, but this was especially so in the early 1980s. Two things made Penticton's new 7-Eleven even more exciting for me. First, my parents' fitness studio was only two doors down from it, giving me frequent opportunities to buy their hot dogs, Big Gulps and Slurpees. I exploited this familiarity with 7-Eleven's products to good effect with my classmates at school, feigning nonchalance as I pointedly let it be known that I was a regular there. Second, 7-Eleven had a promotional deal with *Return of the Jedi* to offer Slurpees in a variety of *Jedi*-themed plastic cups. I collected them all, predictably. Even when that promotion ended, 7-Eleven continued to have *Star Wars* connections for me. The store had the Atari *Star Wars* arcade game in it for the entire summer of 1984. I spent hours playing it at 25 cents a pop. I became quite good, good enough that other kids in the store would crowd around to watch me if I was doing well. The admiration of other boys was novel and exhilarating. I imagined this was what it felt like to play hockey like John DeHart or soccer like Dave Sidhu.

Return of the Jedi is easily the least loved of the three original films. There is reason for this. The dialogue is noticeably inferior to *Empire*, and perhaps even to *Star Wars*. Han Solo in particular is given some pretty awful lines—not quite *Holiday Special* awful, but awful by any ordinary measure. Nevertheless I thoroughly enjoy *Jedi* even when I watch it today. The opening sequence, in which Vader arrives in a shuttle at the still-under-construction Death Star and is greeted by a visibly terrified commander, is impressive. Our first sight of Skywalker, choking Gamorrean guards with the same gesture Vader used in the first two films, nicely foreshadows the choice he must make in the film's climax. The introduction of Ian McDiarmid as the Emperor is masterful—the character's emergence from the background of the first two films for the grand finale works very well, due mostly to McDiarmid's genuinely creepy performance. Similarly, the decision to bring Jabba the Hutt out of the shadows was a delight for fanatics like me who paid minute attention to those few passing references to him in *Star Wars* and *Empire*. Finally seeing Jabba on screen is one of the things that made *Jedi* so exciting—and why George Lucas was mistaken to add a computer-generated Jabba to the "special edition" version of *Star Wars* many years later. The build-up to the film's climactic battle sequences, alternating between the frenetic space battle over Endor, the noisy melee on its surface below and the quiet, eerily uneventful interview between Skywalker and Palpatine on the Death Star, creates an oddly pleasurable sort of stress for the viewer. *Return of the Jedi* has its share of detractors, and I understand the arguments against it: the unoriginality of a second Death Star, the cloying cuteness of the Ewoks, the ignominious death of Boba Fett, the improbable pointlessness of Luke and Leia being siblings, and more. But none of this bothered me when I was ten, and none of it bothers me much now.

I saw *Jedi* in the theatre several times. The Pen-Mar ran ads in the *Penticton Herald* announcing that the film had been held over for a second week, then a third, and a fourth, fifth, sixth, seventh. Finally after eight weeks it exhausted its audience and was replaced by *Mr. Mom* or *Staying Alive* or *Krull* or some such thing. And that was it. The story was told, the trilogy was complete, *Return of the Jedi* had left town and George Lucas had said publicly he had no plans to make any more films in the series any time soon. Though it was not immediately apparent to me, given the continuing bombardment of *Star-Wars*-themed toys, junk food, video games, trading cards and novelty items of every kind, the spring of 1983 was the beginning of an end for me. Gradually I was starting my move away from *Star Wars* and towards other interests.

*

Star Wars did not fade quickly. The release of *Jedi* in May 1983 gave it momentum through Christmas and into the following year. Kenner helped somewhat by delaying the release of its Emperor and Wicket figures until 1984, thus artificially prolonging its audience's enthusiasm. But even a film as successful as *Return of the*

Jedi eventually leaves the theatres. And without the promise of future instalments, interest in the franchise began to decline. Not my interest—not by 1984 at any rate. But the market for *Star Wars* as a whole began to contract. I was keenly aware of this at the time. There were many signs: fewer television commercials for Kenner *Star Wars* toys; fewer of the toys themselves in the shops, and placed less prominently on the shelves than in the past; fewer pages devoted to *Star Wars* toys and merchandise in the Sears catalogue and other print advertisements; the disappearance of tie-ins at 7-Eleven and elsewhere; and an intangible aura of familiarity, bleeding into mild contempt, that increasingly hung over everything to do with *Star Wars*.

The clearest sign of decline, to my eleven-year-old eyes, was the rise of challengers, and ultimately successors, to *Star Wars*'s previously indisputable leadership of the boys' toy and entertainment markets. *Masters of the Universe*, *G.I. Joe* and *Transformers* were the three great rivals to *Star Wars*'s dominance, especially on the action figure front. By 1984, all three of these franchises had an enormous advantage: each was producing new content, be it television shows, comic books or just new toys. *Star Wars*, by contrast, was atrophying. It is no wonder that the boys at school, especially those in grades below me, were turning their attention to these things. None of them ever interested me in the slightest. On the contrary, I harboured a quiet resentment of them. I could see what they were doing. They were displacing, even replacing *Star Wars*. I would not participate in that. I stayed with *Star Wars* like a captain going down with his ship.

It was not only my sense of loyalty that turned me against these upstarts. They simply did not speak to me. I had never cared much for cars, so *Transformers* left me cold. I had a visceral distaste for He-Man—his comic-book muscularity and near-total nudity struck me as obscene, a prudery I likely inherited from my mother. Beyond these superficial objections stood the fact that none of these new crazes came with compelling stories. *Star Wars* was not about swords and spaceships and explosions. It was about things that could not easily be successfully imitated. There was a story behind it, a real story, not just a plot on which to drape special effects and merchandise like clothes on a hanger. Without a story, these would-be replacements of *Star Wars* were anaemic.

But it may be that I was judging them too hastily, for the truth is I never really gave them much of a try. The comic books and Saturday morning cartoons for *G.I. Joe*, *Transformers* and *Masters of the Universe* were all, ultimately, vehicles for the sale of toys, and by age eleven I was not really playing with toys anymore. I did not even play with the *Star Wars* toys I continued to ask for and buy. I still wanted them, but having acquired them I admired them briefly then filed them away with the rest of my plastic treasures, arranged neatly in their cases and boxes in my bedroom closet. I had gone from a child who played with *Star Wars* toys to a pre-pubescent who collected them.

Lucasfilm must have detected this shift in its audience's key demographic, for by late 1984 it was beginning to generate *Star Wars* spin-offs for a younger, more lucrative market. George Lucas made, or allowed to be made, two television specials featuring the franchise's most self-consciously cutesy creation, the Ewoks. The programs, *The Ewok Adventure* (1984) (later released in Europe as *Caravan of Courage*) and *Ewoks: the Battle for Endor* (1985), both featured children and Ewoks as the main characters, although *Battle for Endor* added the Quaker Oats man, Wilford Brimley. Lucasfilm again pitched to children in 1985 with two animated series, *Star Wars: Ewoks* and *Star Wars: Droids*, both of which were shown on Saturday mornings with no pretension of being anything but children's programming. Despite my continued infatuation with *Star Wars*, I paid little attention to these programs. I had looked forward to ABC's airing of *The Ewok Adventure* on 25 November

1984 but was disappointed by what I saw. There were no Jedi, no stormtroopers, almost nothing to connect the show to what I knew of *Star Wars* except the Ewoks themselves. After that initial letdown, the cartoons and the second Ewok special failed to excite my interest. No one else seemed much interested either.

Star Wars was finally running out of steam. It had enjoyed an extraordinary run, but it was coming to an end. The television specials and cartoons were at best half-hearted efforts to keep the phenomenon alive, and were unfit for the task. No other efforts were mounted. *Star Wars* was dying off without great resistance from either its creators or its fans.

*

There remained one small corner of the *Star Wars* universe that endeavoured to keep the flame alive. Marvel Comics Group had begun publishing a monthly *Star Wars* comic book in spring 1977, breaking the film into a six-issue series. The first two instalments were prepared before the final edit of *Star Wars* was completed. The books' writer and illustrator, who had not seen the film, relied on sketches, camera stills and early versions of the script to prepare their adaptation. This explains how these first two issues came to include scenes that did not make it into the final cut of the film, such as Luke's conversation with Biggs Darklighter about joining the rebellion. It does not appear to explain, however, why Darth Vader's helmet is green on the cover of the self-proclaimed "FABULOUS FIRST ISSUE". The six Marvel *Star Wars* comics were, like all things *Star Wars*, hugely successful, so that there was never any serious question of whether to continue the comic after issue six. By the time *Return of the Jedi* was released, some 85 issues had appeared. The challenge for Marvel from May 1983 onwards was to keep telling a story in print which its creator had clearly brought to an end on film.

Marvel *Star Wars* comics were perhaps the only aspect of the *Star Wars* phenomenon that had not reached me by the time *Jedi* was released. I was too young for comic books in 1977, *Star Wars* or otherwise. It was not until late 1984 that I discovered Marvel *Star Wars* and comic books in general. I was milling about the 7-Eleven, killing time as I waited for my mother to finish work at the Base. I blithely spun the store's three-sided, wire comic book rack, not looking for anything in particular. And there was Marvel *Star Wars* number 90, "THE CHOICE!" The asking price was 60 cents US, 75 cents Canadian, 30 pence UK. The titular choice was Princess Leia's: don a gown and tackle matters of state with the likes of Mon Mothma and Admiral Ackbar, or don a flight suit and blaster to gallivant around the universe brandishing arms with her brother Luke and lover Han? This sartorial dilemma did not much move me, but there was precious little *Star Wars* about anymore. I took what I could get. At a cost of three rounds of Atari *Star Wars*, I bought the book. As with any first-time comic book reading experience, I found the story somewhat bewildering. It assumed I had read the previous issue, and a few more previous to that, which I had not. It assumed I was familiar with characters not found in the movies, which I was not. But it was sufficiently entertaining that I bought the next issue, "Wookie World", in which Han and Chewbacca travel to the Wookie homeworld "Kazhyyyk" (as Marvel spelled it) and Chewie's son Lumpy, of *Holiday Special* infamy, makes another appearance.

Only days after buying this issue, I was wandering up Martin Street one afternoon when I came across something I had never seen before. In a narrow storefront retail space connected from the inside to the Penticton Inn hotel was a shop displaying comic books in the window. I went in. The shop was dark, small and silent. There was no one there but a tall, red-haired, red-moustachioed, slightly-pudgy-around-the-middle, thirty-something man seated behind a glass display-case to my left. To my right was a wall of shelves displaying nothing but comic books. Straight ahead was a simple, wooden, rectangular case, about chest-high on me, full of more comic books, these ones sorted alphabetically and individually stored in clear plastic bags. I had never seen, or even heard of, anything like this place, and I was not entirely sure what it was.

"Hello," said the man behind the counter with mild sarcasm intended more to break my slack-jawed silence than to welcome me.

"Is this a…comic book shop?" I stammered, ignoring his greeting. He confirmed that it was. I told him that I had never seen one before, which must have been obvious. He replied that there was one in Kelowna. He might as well have said Kampala; other than visits to Dallas, I had hardly ever left town. I asked him if he had *Star Wars*, although I had no intention of buying as I had just picked up what I believed to be the latest issue from 7-Eleven. He directed me to the S section of the shelves to my right. And there was Marvel *Star Wars* number 92, "The Dream", a special double-sized issue featuring gorgeous cover art by Cynthia Martin and Bill Sienkiewicz. 7-Eleven didn't even have this yet. I was amazed. I grabbed it, spun around, advanced three paces and presented the book at the counter to pay. The man rang me through an outmoded, yellowed till and said, "You know I'm not actually open yet".

This was Bob, and that was Bob's Comics. I was Bob's first customer. For the next six years, until I graduated from high school and left town, Bob was a central figure in my life. When Bob and I met, I had all the prerequisites of a consummate nerd: I was a bright, self-conscious, uncoordinated, bookishly-inclined eleven year old boy with an unshakeable interest in three movies which, taken together, I had probably seen fifty times. But I was not a nerd yet. To reach true nerdiness, to attain Nerdvana, I needed Bob.

It was not the mere reading of comic books that made a boy a nerd. Nor was *Star-Wars*-mania enough—it had been, after all, nearly universal amongst the boys of my age until about 1984, and was common enough amongst the girls, too. The difference between me pre-Bob and the existential status of nerdiness I attained through Bob was an obsession with trivial and (in many cases) wholly imaginary details about subjects which ordinary people either ignored entirely or regarded as inconsequential diversions. A typical book enthusiast will read Tolkein's *Lord of the Rings* novels and take great pleasure in them, perhaps even re-reading them several times. A nerd will read the books, commit to memory as much detail about the characters, the story, the settings and the action as the author himself provided, amplify this detail with his own speculations and fantasies, then regale his listeners with this minutiae at every opportunity as if it were actual knowledge of something useful. The mastery of insignificant or even purely fabricated information, the achievement of professorial erudition about things that do not in fact exist or, if they do exist, barely matter, is the true hallmark of a nerd.

Bob's Comics was a standing invitation to the children of Penticton to become nerds. I accepted— although not by becoming a devotee of the Marvel or DC universes, like most of the teenage and quasi-adult nerds I got to know through Bob. My nerdiness took a related, but somewhat milder form. I was not obsessed with the fantasy worlds related in comic books; my interest in the stories was real but moderate. Instead, I became infatuated with the burgeoning world of comic book collecting. Before Bob, I read one comic book for entertainment. After Bob, I hoarded hundreds of comic books out of infatuation, cupidity and speculation. Bob ushered me (and cashiered me) into a world of Mylar sleeves, acid-free backing boards, Overstreet price guides, comic book grading schemes and speculative trading. Marvel *Star Wars* was the gateway. When I first entered Bob's Comics I only wanted the latest issue, but once I discovered the possibility of buying back issues I had to have the entire run. Next I had to have the entire run in mint or near-mint condition. After that I began collecting other comic book titles, less out of interest in the stories themselves as the narcissism of collecting for its own sake. When, in the summer of 1986, Marvel abruptly cancelled *Star Wars* only a few months after cutting the book back to bi-monthly publication in response to falling sales, I was disappointed. But by then I was a nerd. I kept collecting comics.

*

I picked up another prototypically nerdy pastime at about this time. My mother had a work associate of some kind whose son Dean was no more than two years older than me but seemed to me to be practically a grown man. It was the difference between pre-pubescence and full-on puberty—he talked dirty, read dirty books when he could find them, was at least a head taller than me, and lacked the doe-eyed innocence that still marked me as a child. Dean's mother was a single mum with little money (as my own mother was soon to become) and their home bore similarities to our motel house: it was cheap, run down, near the beach (Skaha Beach—the southernmost of Penticton's two glorious beaches), and formed part of a slightly seedy housing complex. Dean had friends in the complex who, like him, were older than me and, like the surroundings, were a bit shabby. They all had acne in varying degrees of horribleness, and a few had thin man-boy moustaches which their parents allowed them to cultivate when any aesthetically sensitive mother or father would have insisted on immediate removal. All these boys were keenly interested in sex, violence and other forms of luridness. One of them shocked me soon after we met with a large, well-drawn pencil sketch of the comic strip character Garfield the Cat sporting an enormous erection. These boys, none of whose names I remember apart from Dean, were wholly unlike Nathan Barlow or any of the other boys I had ever known. They were crude, racy, low and nasty. I thought they were great. And it was through them that I was introduced to *Dungeons and Dragons*.

Star Wars and *Dungeons and Dragons* have some striking similarities. They are near-perfect contemporaries: in the early 1970s, as George Lucas was dreaming up the plot to his space fantasy film in California, Dave Arneson and Gary Gygax were writing the rules for their mediaeval fantasy game in Wisconsin. Both phenomena were met with near-fatal scepticism from existing outlets: Lucas repeatedly failed to interest studios in a film they did not understand, while Gygax and Arneson ultimately resorted to self-publishing a game traditional publishers rejected because there appeared to be no way to win it. Despite these initial setbacks, both *Star Wars* and *Dungeons and Dragons* quickly became massively successful and near-universally known, even amongst people who took no interest in them. The success of both creations depended in large part on their ability to captivate people's imaginations and persuade their audiences to believe in implausible, even faintly ridiculous fantasy worlds.

The clear leader of Dean's gang of pubescent lowlifes was the Garfield pornographer—a short, chunky, hairy, Varigray-bespectacled bugbear of a boy who, naturally, discharged the duties of Dungeon Master. All the rulebooks, modules, dice, painted lead figurines and other paraphernalia we needed to play the game belonged to him, although he did not pay much attention to any of it. Instead of memorizing and fussing over the rules, as most nerds did, Garfield concerned himself only with the roleplaying element of the game— the creation of fantastic worlds and adventures for his players. Playing *Dungeons and Dragons* with Garfield was like interviewing a schizophrenic. He loved voices, which he performed with deranged zeal. He loved characters and drama, but knew to temper these aspects of the game with an appreciation of his audience, meaning four or five 13- to 15-year-old boys who would quickly lose patience with an overly drawn out or subtle story. Garfield was an excellent Dungeon Master because he was a natural performer. The game gave him a stage.

I spent much of that summer playing D&D with Dean and his gang. It was a terrific introduction to the most important part of the game, namely the roleplaying. But it was a lousy introduction to the rules. Being a novice player who did not own any of the rulebooks, I was mostly ignorant of how the game was supposed to work. I just rolled dice when I was told to. But I was taken with *Dungeons and Dragons*. Later that year my mother took my sister and me with her on a business trip to the States where I stumbled across a toy store that sold D&D books. I begged mum for the US$12 needed to buy a copy of the *Players Handbook*. For the next two months I spent every spare waking moment poring over it. Garfield had simplified things, even got things wildly wrong. Just because you're a sixth level magic user didn't mean you could cast sixth level spells! And so on. I was grateful to Garfield for introducing me to the game, but now I wanted to play it right.

Perhaps the greater revelation I took from the *Players Handbook* was Gary Gygax's writing. Looking back now, his prose frequently strikes me as overwrought, pretentious, even silly. But I cannot hold it against him because at thirteen years old I loved it. I had never read anything like it. Where else could I have found passages like, "Loyalty Base simply shows the subtraction from or addition to the henchman's and other servitors' loyalty (q.v.) scores", or "The Astral Plane radiates from the Prime Material to a non-space where endless vortices spiral to the parallel Prime Material Planes and to the Outer Planes as well"? Often I had to read and re-read, and sometimes I still did not understand. But I was not deterred. Gygax's writing style conveyed a sense of initiation into mystery that perfectly matched what I imagined *Dungeons and Dragons* to be—a sort of secret society of erudite fantasists. Of course you had to work at it. And there was more to Gygax's style than its not-infrequent florid passages, its self-seriousness, its patina of hackneyed historical and political insights. Gygax also wrote with conspicuous, infectious enthusiasm for his topic. "This game lets all of your fantasies come true", he proclaimed. "This is a world where monsters, dragons, good and evil high priests, fierce demons, and even the gods themselves may enter your character's life. Enjoy, for this game is what dreams are made of!!" Wonderful.

Finally, after some nine years of single-minded devotion to one pastime, I was developing new interests: comic books and *Dungeons and Dragons*. These were not particularly constructive or socially commendable hobbies. My interest in them certainly did not improve my fitness or contribute to my community in any fashion, though I am convinced that D&D broadened my mind in lasting ways. But whether these nerdy pursuits were good or bad when measured on their own, there was at least one positive thing to be said for them: they were not *Star Wars*. I was, at last, moving on.

*

In September 1986, aged thirteen, I began grade eight at Penticton Senior Secondary School, known to all as Pen Hi. My entrance into adolescence was complete: I was officially a teenager. That the decline, indeed the near disappearance, of *Star Wars* as a pop culture phenomenon coincided so perfectly with the onset of my adolescence was not, I think, coincidence. It was simple demographics: the mainstay of *Star Wars*'s fan base was evaporating. Every surviving three to five year old boy in the world who loved *Star Wars* in 1977 was now a teenager. All those little action-figure-fanciers and trading-card-collectors were now turning their attentions to teenage boy concerns: being cool, attracting girls and attracting girls.

(Some of these boys must have been interested in attracting other boys, not girls, but I never heard a word of it. This was the 1980s after all. A Pen Hi friend of mine who, years later, came out as gay told me that throughout high school he thought homosexuals were men who wore women's clothing. My notion was more ridiculous still—I used to fear that maybe I was gay because I sometimes preferred to sit rather than stand when urinating.)

The defining film of teenage life in the mid-1980s was not, of course, *Star Wars* or its sequels. It was *The Breakfast Club*. That film's easy stereotypes of adolescent forms—the jock, the nerd, the headbanger, the princess, the outcast—seemed to me to reflect reality, although in truth they probably shaped it. If the film's message was that these socially-accepted constructions of adolescent existence were artificial, that message did not get through to the teenagers of Pen Hi. Instead, we all agreed, in an unspoken way, to try to fit ourselves into these categories. I was no athlete, and I did not smoke or drink or break things, so jock and headbanger were out. That left nerd and outcast. I probably would have preferred outcast, which at least had a bit of romance to it, but I was a rotten skateboarder. Meanwhile my grades were good, I was an avid comic book collector, and *Dungeons and Dragons* was spurring me on to read books about history and mythology. Nerd it was.

Bob wanted to attend a comic book convention in Penticton. The difficulty was that there were no comic book conventions in Penticton. Bob's solution was that I should organize one. Somehow he talked me into it, and before long I found myself in the lobby of the Sandman Hotel asking the receptionist how to book a conference room. I drew posters by hand, made copies on the photocopier at my mother's office, and hung them around town. Bob spread the word to comic shop owners and private collectors he knew in the surrounding towns, and before long I was selling tables and collecting admission ($1) at the door. I made a little money and thought it was pretty neat. More importantly, I met Scott Barillaro. He stopped me in the hallway outside Pen Hi's library about a week or so before the event. "You're the guy running the convention, right?" Right. "Bob told me about you. You play D&D?"

That was all it took. Scott no doubt saw in me what I saw in him: a fellow nerd. I was mildly taken aback, in the three or four interactions that followed this brief encounter, by how Scott seemed to regard me as a firm friend, or at least a dependable ally, when we barely knew each other. But Scott was right. There was no foreplay in this relationship; our nerd-love was consummated in the time it took to cast a Fireball spell: three segments. Twenty-two years later he had my fiancée's wedding band in his pocket as I tied my necktie, fastened my cufflinks and otherwise prepared myself to walk down an improvised aisle in an Okanagan orchard and take marriage vows. All because Bob was too lazy, or too clever, to organize his own comic book convention.

Scott and I made our way through high school together. The things that first attracted us to each other, comic books and *Dungeons and Dragons*, occupied a lot of our time. There were dozens of Friday and Saturday nights spent playing D&D from 5 p.m. until 2 in the morning or later: me, Scott, Sissy Bobo, and one or two others sitting around the dining room table at our house rolling dice and making believe until one of us—nearly always me—fell asleep. When, in 1987, West End Games published *Star Wars: The Roleplaying Game*, I immediately instructed Bob to order a copy of every book, supplement and boxed miniatures set the company made. (Bob had added roleplaying games to his shop, at my urging, not long before. He knew nothing about them.) Scott, Sissy and I all liked the game and played it often. It was well-designed, its lead miniatures were strangely small but very attractive, and the *Star Wars* story readily lent itself to tabletop roleplaying. But this was the only bit of *Star Wars* that regularly impinged upon my consciousness in the late 1980s. Literally and figuratively, I had put the rest of it away.

As Scott and I got older, our friendship expanded into areas outside the nerdosphere: our schoolwork, troubles with our parents (mine had finally divorced, his were heading that way), plans for the future, and girls. Against all odds, we both found ourselves with fairly serious girlfriends by age seventeen. We were crazy about them, but finding time for all-night roleplaying sessions became increasingly difficult when confronted with our girlfriends' expectations and, more to the point, our own libidos. The problem went beyond scheduling, for me at least. I started to feel self-conscious about my nerdy pastimes. I do not remember my girlfriend, Emma, ever expressly discouraging them. But she was a brilliant, very serious-minded girl whose own spare time was spent obtaining her grade ten piano certificate from the Royal Conservatory of Music, playing bassoon in the local orchestra, and visiting the campuses of famous universities. I assumed that she must disapprove of my comic book collecting and my all-night cheese-puff-and-root-beer-fuelled giant-slaying sessions with Scott and Sissy. I still liked these things, but I also liked her and wanted her to like me. So I played down my geeky side and played up my quite genuine interest in the things she exposed me to: the high school debating club, literature, and choosing a university. (Scott never felt any such diffidence. His girlfriend knew very well what a geek he was. What kept Scott away from D&D at my house on Friday nights was that, unlike me, he was actually getting laid.)

As the 1980s came to a close and I approached my high school graduation, I finally came to see the absurdity in the *Breakfast Club* categorization of teenagers. I began to understand the transitoriness of adolescence—that it was just a phase I had to go through before sloughing off childhood for good and getting on with the rest of my life. I got a job at a used bookshop the owner of which, Bruce, was a film and literature buff—as keen on Kurosawa as Bob was on Captain America. I studied hard, did well and won a place at McGill, one of the best universities in the country. I graduated from Pen Hi in June 1991. Towards the end of the summer I packed up my room in the house my grandparents had helped my mother buy five years earlier and prepared for the move to Montreal. Stored away neatly in the back of my bedroom's deep closet was my *Star Wars* collection: the action figures, the playsets, the books, the trading cards, the full-colour prints, the plastic 7-Eleven cups, the Princess Leia bubble bath, and all sorts of other odds and ends. It took seven cardboard boxes to pack them all away. I carefully marked each box in black felt pen: Gib's *Star Wars* collection. Not for a second did I consider getting rid of these things. But I certainly was not bringing them with me. They were childhood keepsakes, not things of current importance. *Star Wars* was a fond memory.

TURMOIL IN THE REPUBLIC

I look out the window of my small room in R Staircase. The gardens below are still. The sky is bright and clear. I won't need my coat. I head out, down into the gardens, through the arched passageway into Chapel Court and on to the porters' lodge where I am meeting Greg. It is March 1997, I have just turned 24, and Greg and I are going to a matinee showing of *Star Wars*.

Greg is a doctoral student in German philosophy with particular interest in Friedrich Nietzsche. I read a lot of Nietzsche at McGill and am interested in Greg's work, but he does not willingly talk about it. In my short time in Britain, I have learned that the British abhor 'shop talk'. Instead, as we make our way up Sidney Street to the bus stop and onward to a cinema I have never been to, we trade hollow witticisms and jokey allusions, trying to make them seem effortless when, in my case at least, they are quite the opposite. Greg excels at this game. It is nearly his only form of verbal communication. I try to keep up, and sometimes I do, but mostly I feel as though I am hanging on by my fingertips. When, rarely, I manage a decent quip or successful riposte, Greg smirks silently and turns his eyes to the ground. I am immensely gratified by this acknowledgement and will replay the scene in my mind later.

I am what is known, in the peculiar jargon of Cambridge, as a lawyer. In fact I am no more than a first-year law student, and not an especially promising one at that, but in Cambridge the medical students are medics, the mathematics students are mathmos, the natural science students are natscis and the law students are lawyers. Law is an undergraduate course in Cambridge, but as I already have a BA from McGill my college has accorded me membership in the Middle Combination Room (the organization representing graduate students) and in practice I spend as much or more time with graduate students like Greg as with the 17- and 18-year-olds in my course. Certainly I would only go see *Star Wars* with a graduate student; the undergrads would not understand the significance of the event. But Greg is my age and his childhood, like mine, was shaped by the films. The fact that he is British and grew up thousands of miles away from me makes no difference.

The re-appearance of *Star Wars* in my consciousness in the spring of 1997 broke the longest *Star-Wars*-free spell my life had ever known, dating from my entrance into university in 1991 if not earlier. During that time I had thrown myself completely into the life of the mind. If I was not attending a lecture in European history or Greek philosophy or English literature I was studying these topics with a monastic devotion in a carrel at the McLennan library. The various dingy apartments I occupied in the McGill student ghetto—a different one every year—were crammed with library books, textbooks and second-hand treasures acquired during my near-daily visits to The Word, a poky bookshop in the heart of the Ghetto which was so well known to students and bibliophiles that it did not even have a sign out front. On my desk, at my bedside or ranged carefully away in IKEA Billy bookcases were Plato, Aristotle, Descartes, Kant, Hegel, Nietzsche, Weber, Shakespeare, Donne, Gogol, Tolstoy, Twain, Yeats, Pound, Stevens, Walcott and so many others, without even mentioning the profusion of historical works on ancient Greece, Tudor-Stuart England, the Great War, Russian communism, or the history of Christian thought.

Whenever I could afford the time—usually not until after final exams—I brought my copy of the *Riverside Shakespeare* to the audio-visual library, borrowed a BBC Television production of a Shakespeare play on VHS, and spent four hours or so reading along as I took in the magnificent performances of Derek Jacobi, John Gielgud and the rest.

Comic books, *Dungeons and Dragons* and *Star Wars* had no place in this new world I had entered. I found my former interest in them slightly embarrassing. When, in September 1992, my best friend Scott transferred to McGill and became my roommate, he brought a copy of a *Star Wars* novel by Timothy Zahn called *Heir to the Empire*. He said it was good. Many people agreed, and the book spawned a new category of *Star Wars* content now known as the Expanded Universe. I didn't even pick it up. Why spend my precious time on it when I could be reading *The Brothers Karamazov* or *The Nicomachean Ethics* or any of the thousands of great works of literature and philosophy I had not yet discovered? These works loomed over me, a giant checklist of intellectual accomplishment upon which I had hardly made a mark. And what would Emma—the same brilliant, supremely talented girlfriend I had in high school, and who arrived at McGill at the same time as Scott—think to see me wasting my time on *Star Wars* again? So I did not read *Heir to the Empire* or its sequels. I did not go along with Scott when he joined the university's D&D club (whose office was just next door to that of the Debating Union, which I did join). I did not buy any of the new Dark Horse *Star Wars* comics that began appearing at this time. All this was behind me. I had become a man, and put away childish things.

And yet here I was, now 24 years old, studying law at an ancient university, and instead of spending the morning lounging in the college gardens reading about the British constitution or public international law, I was on a bus to see *Star Wars* with a British Nietzsche scholar. I had not changed much. I was still a serious, ambitious student. I still read Shakespeare for pleasure. But I was coming to see that my understanding of maturity was itself immature. The British students' distaste for shop talk, for talking about ideas at all, was exaggerated. At times it bordered on anti-intellectual. I found it silly, even frustrating, that if I wanted to have a serious conversation over lunch in Hall I had to sit with the other foreign students. But this British affectation of indifference towards the things they had come to university to study proved to be a boon to me. I never doubted the intelligence of the British students. They had been admitted into Cambridge, after all, and besides that so many of them sparkled with talent and ability. So when I found myself chatting with them in the college pub, or dining with them at formal dinners, their low-brow enthusiasms—for TV chat shows, Premiership football, the Spice Girls, *The Simpsons*, and a thousand other interests the characters of *Brideshead Revisited* never indulged in—elevated these things in my esteem. I began to rediscover a truth I had known as a 13-year-old *Dungeons and Dragons* nerd: intelligence and frivolous pastimes were not mutually exclusive; on the contrary, they frequently went hand-in-hand. I had traded my childhood infatuation with *Star Wars* for a barely-postpubescent infatuation with scholarly learning. Just as I had allowed my obsession with *Star Wars* to crowd out other interests as a child, I had, in university, excluded all other facets of life as inconsistent with bookishness and intellectual improvement. There was a middle ground between these positions which I never seemed to occupy.

It may not have been a coincidence that Emma and I finally broke up around the time I came to this realization. Our devotion to each other had been remarkable. We stayed together during my first year at McGill, despite the fact that she was completing high school in Penticton four thousand kilometres away. She then came to McGill and our relationship continued. While it appeared to all the world that she had followed me there, it was more a case of me following her: after touring numerous universities with her parents well before her sixteenth birthday, she had decided on McGill and recommended it to me. I was attracted to McGill in large part because I knew Emma would be there. We continued dating throughout our McGill years and then decided together on law at Sidney Sussex College, Cambridge. (I was inclined towards Oxford but allowed her to bring me around. She later did a master's degree there and told me, to my slight annoyance, how much better she liked it.) It was not long after arriving in Cambridge that we began drifting apart. Emma met an Englishman who was even more bookish (and considerably smarter) than me. I met an exchange student from Yale with dual manias for English literature and the Spice Girls. When finally we admitted to ourselves that we were through, the question that had dominated my decision-making for nearly seven years—what would Emma think?—lost some of its potency. Now, if I wanted to see *Star Wars* at the matinee, I could, in theory, do so without worrying what my girlfriend Emma would make of it. (In fact I did continue to worry about the answer to this question, at least a little, for years after we broke up.)

So Greg and I went to see *Star Wars*. But what we saw was not quite the *Star Wars* we knew. For this "special edition", George Lucas had added effects and even entirely new scenes. Some of these changes I appreciated, such as the shot of the Millennium Falcon escaping Mos Eisley, or that of Rebel fighters assembling before their assault on the Death Star. These updates enhanced the story without changing it, adding gorgeous effects that did not detract from or impede the existing narrative. But other changes were troubling. The infamous addition of an improbably errant close-range shot by Jabba's lieutenant, Greedo, prior to Han's murder of him in the Mos Eisley cantina was surprising and annoying, but did not greatly exercise me at the time. In retrospect, however, I agree with the "Han Shot First" agitators who have made their voices heard through countless movie reviews, t-shirts and web sites over the years. What I really objected to was the addition of Jabba the Hutt, inserted by means of computer-generated imagery and cutting-room-floor material which ought to have stayed there. Not only does Jabba come off as a buffoon instead of a threat as he slithers around Docking Bay 94, but the whole notion of him being ambulatory at all bothered me. Much of what made him sinister and repulsive in *Return of the Jedi* was that he barely moved; he was the exemplar of sloth and avarice. I preferred Lucas's treatment of Jabba in the original theatrical releases of *Star Wars* and

Empire: a shadowy, threatening figure from Solo's past or, to invoke a Lucas phrase, a phantom menace.

Despite these complaints, I enjoyed seeing *Star Wars* again. When the special editions of the two sequels were released in the UK, Greg and I made the same trip to the cinema, in April for *Empire* and May for *Jedi*. The changes to *Empire* were few and unobjectionable. But the addition of a Muppets-inspired miniature music video to the Jabba's Palace sequence of *Jedi* was horrifying. It communicated to me that Lucas and I were suddenly in profound disagreement about what kind of story *Star Wars* was. This scene, more than any other change brought by the special editions, made me despair for the possibility that Lucas could pull off successful precursors (or, as Lucas dubbed them, "prequels") to the original trilogy. Lucas's intention of making the first, second and third episodes of his tale was known by 1997. The special editions, though purportedly released to celebrate the twentieth anniversary of *Star Wars*, were surely motivated instead by the desire to build interest in the coming films. As we walked out of the theatre and into the sunlight of an English May day, Greg and I shared our reservations about what we had seen. His criticism of the new *Jedi* and what it said about Lucas's vision was even fiercer than mine. Despite the muppetry, I maintained some hope that the coming films would succeed. Lucas was, after all, the creator of *Star Wars*. How far wrong could he stray?

*

The phone rings. I am sitting at an improvised desk in a small suite of offices on the third floor of Centre Block, Parliament Buildings, Ottawa. I am wearing one of two suits I bought before leaving England. They are the only ones I have. I steel myself. It is my job to answer the phone if, as today, no one else is around. I must, of course, answer in French; no one calling the office of a Quebec separatist member of parliament expects to be greeted in English, even by the underpaid intern. The greeting is not the hard part. What can be tricky is understanding what the caller wants. My French is fairly good for someone who grew up in the resolutely Anglophone interior of British Columbia. But understanding what someone is saying to you over a telephone line is, I have learned, rather more difficult than understanding what someone is saying to you when looking you in the eye. Usually I manage well enough, but when things go badly they go very badly. If I hesitate, or misspeak, or misunderstand, the caller's confusion inflames the situation. I can almost hear him or her thinking, "Why is an Anglo answering the phone at the office of the Bloc Québécois's foreign affairs critic? Who is this person? Have I dialled the wrong number? *C'est quoi cet osti de merde là?*"

The phone rings again. I pick it up and pronounce my boss's name with exaggerated confidence. The voice on the other end laughs and says, in faultless English, "That cracks me up every time". It's Pat, a fellow parliamentary intern.

I bristle. "We're not all perfectly bilingual, you know."

"It's just funny that you're there at all. You're no Quebec separatist. Anyway, you're not going to believe what happened. There was a contest on the radio this morning. I won two tickets to *The Phantom Menace*, opening night—tonight. Do you want to go?"

Of course I do. I am about to say so. Then I remember the plans I made with Andy, a friend from McGill who, coincidentally, ended up in Cambridge at the same time as me and now lives in Ottawa. Andy, like Scott, Greg, Pat and just about every other man I know between twenty-five and thirty, grew up consumed by *Star Wars* mania. Andy and I had not even tried to get opening night tickets—we assumed it would be hopeless. Instead we bought tickets for the next night, Thursday, 20 May 1999. We had been talking about seeing the new *Star Wars* film together for weeks now. I explained my predicament to Pat.

"Just go with Andy again tomorrow night. Seriously—you can't say no." Pat was right. This was too good to pass up. But it somehow felt disloyal to Andy. It briefly occurred to me that I need not tell him—I could just go with him on Thursday as if I had never seen the film before. I immediately thought of the IG-88 rifle I stole from Nathan, and the *Making of Star Wars* library book I never returned. No—my days of *Star-Wars*-inspired dishonesty were over. I was twenty-six years old for Christ's sake. I would just have to explain the situation to Andy. He would understand. And I would still go with him tomorrow night. I would see *The Phantom Menace* twice.

I left work as soon as I could, changed clothes, ate a quick dinner and headed to the cinema to meet Pat. Our tickets were for 7 o'clock. There was a crowd of joyous, excited people—mostly men around our age—waiting to be admitted. A few were in amateurish costumes but most wore casual clothes appropriate to a May evening in Ottawa: jeans and a t-shirt, maybe with a light jacket. Waiting in line, Pat and I compared what we had heard about the film from the early reviews, almost all of which had been negative. Strangers within earshot of us in the queue joined our conversation without hesitation—a behaviour I had frequently observed in public places in the US but rarely in Canada. There was something festive in the air that suspended the usual rules of Canadian social conduct. The consensus among our fellow fans was that the original *Star Wars* got bad reviews, too, but nevertheless went on to be the most successful film of all time. George Lucas would not disappoint us. We were about to be told a grand story—again.

At long last the doors opened. The patrons filed in, in high spirits but not unruly—this was a Canadian crowd, after all. Pat and I found quite good seats: only slightly to the right of centre and about half-way back. We sat down and waited. The lights stayed up and the screen stayed blank. I was growing impatient. Then I recalled how long I had waited for the sequel to *The Empire Strikes Back*. Compared to that, this was nothing. Before I had a chance to share this comforting thought with Pat, the lights went down, prompting a roar from the crowd. But it was a false alarm: seemingly every one of the hundreds of fans surrounding us had forgotten about the trailers. I doubt that trailers have ever received a rockier reception from film-goers than those that preceded *The Phantom Menace* on opening night. Absolutely no one was interested in any other movie. Jokers in the audience heckled the trailers, sometimes with catcalls and *Star Wars* catchphrases ("These are not the droids we're looking for!"). The projectionist was unmoved, however; the agonizing succession of trailer after trailer continued for what seemed like half an hour.

Just when the audience's patience was stretched to the breaking point, the screen fell dark. Was this it? Blackness—but what would follow? When the Twentieth Century Fox logo appeared, with its famous fanfare, the crowd erupted. Then came the fairy-tale words that literally started it all: A long time ago in a galaxy far, far away…and CRASH! goes the orchestra, blasting the *Star Wars* emblem into our chests like a paramedic with a defibrillator. The audience was delirious. While there remained a small voice inside me saying, *You're too old for this* and *Wait and see*, I ignored it and allowed myself to be swept away. *Star Wars* was back. The iconic logo sped away into space and yellow text began to crawl up the screen: Episode I: THE PHANTOM MENACE. "Turmoil has engulfed the Galactic Republic. The taxation of trade routes to outlying star systems is in dispute."

These two sentences startled me with their dissonance. First was their dissonance with each other— how could a dispute over taxation of trade routes to outlying star systems engulf an entire republic in turmoil? Beyond this was their dissonance with *Star*

Wars itself. Intragalactic trade law was not the stuff of my childhood fantasies. How could an epic story start like this? I found myself doubting *The Phantom Menace* less than a minute after it had begun. I was not the only one. The audience around me had fallen mostly silent. This was not a rapt silence. It was a silent foreboding.

*

What followed was two hours of crushing disappointment. *The Phantom Menace* was dreadful. When considered as a single, stand-alone film, it was confusing, gaudy and dull. When considered (as it must be) as a chapter in the *Star Wars* saga, it was worse, for it did violence to some of the fundamental aspects and themes of the story.

The plot was unintelligible. Sitting in the theatre that May evening I truly struggled to understand what I was being told. Why send Jedis to resolve a trade dispute? Why does a blockade of a single planet amount to a galactic crisis? Why is this Qui-Gon Jinn fellow Obi-Wan's mentor when in *The Empire Strikes Back* Obi-Wan told Luke that Yoda trained him? Why is the planet Naboo run by a sixteen-year-old elected queen who speaks like a constipated robot? Why does Jar Jar Binks go to Tatooine? Why is Anakin Skywalker an immaculately conceived slave? Why did Anakin build his mother a protocol droid to help with the housework, and what is the significance of this fact to the story as a whole? Why does the pod race happen? Why did Qui-Gon bet on the race and how did he win? Who is Darth Maul and why is he at odds with Qui-Gon? Why do the Jedi take Anakin away from his mother, abandoning her to a miserable, indentured, childless fate? What are all the parliamentary machinations in the Galactic Senate about? What is the Jedi Council? Why is Yoda so unpleasant with Anakin there? Why were the Naboobs at war with the Gungans and why did they make peace? Why does Qui-Gon hide Anakin in the cockpit of a starfighter, of all places, and how does Anakin manage to operate it? Why do Qui-Gon and Darth Maul die? (From lightsaber wounds, I know, but what purpose do their deaths serve in advancing the story?) Why does the film end when it does? What story has been told from beginning to end?

I left the theatre confounded by these questions. The poor reviews leading up to *The Phantom Menace*, and the disturbing innovations of the "special editions" two years before, had prepared me for the possibility of not liking the film. But I never expected not to understand it. Whether you enjoyed the original three *Star Wars* films or not, you could hardly complain they were too complicated. But this new film simply made no sense to me. I had other complaints, of course. The characters were wooden. The humour was puerile. The special effects seemed more important to the filmmaker than the story. The whole film seemed to take its audience for granted, as if we were bound to approve of it simply because it was *Star Wars*. I found myself involuntarily developing these criticisms in my mind in the days and weeks that followed. But in the immediate aftermath of my first viewing, as Pat and I made our way dejectedly past the long queue of *Star-Wars*-mad fans waiting to be admitted to opening night's late showing, my principal reaction to the film was confusion.

The following night I found myself back at the cinema, this time with Andy. He knew I had seen the film the night before and asked me what I thought. I looked for a way not to answer. I hoped that maybe I had missed something, maybe *The Phantom Menace* was better than I had appreciated, and maybe Andy could show me its merits if only I did not poison his mind with my own prejudice before he saw it for himself. I said only that the film was not what I expected. Andy saw right through these carefully chosen words. Disappointment flashed across his face.

My second viewing of the film in two nights did nothing to lessen my confusion about its plot. Beyond this, I grew angry with George Lucas over parts of *The Phantom Menace* which contradicted aspects, whether express or implied, of the original films. By far the most disappointing break *The Phantom Menace* made with the original trilogy was its elucidation of the Force. The earlier films wisely avoided explaining this mystical phenomenon in any but the broadest of terms. Viewers were left to define, or leave undefined, the mystery of the Force for themselves. In a baffling about-face, *The Phantom Menace* supplanted mystery with quasi-science, explaining the Force as a by-product of the presence of microscopic lifeforms—the so-called midi-chlorians— said to live symbiotically within the cells of other living creatures. The more midi-chlorians inhabit you, the more Force-y you will be. While, in the original trilogy, command of the Force could seemingly be attained by anyone who devoted himself to it, in *The Phantom Menace* Anakin's degree of Force sensitivity was determined by a blood test.

The consequences of this innovation for the moral framework of the *Star Wars* story were, to my mind, ruinous. If, in the original trilogy, the Jedi were an extinct elite, they were nevertheless a meritocratic one, earning their former status through a combination of innate ability and dedication to their discipline. Even a farm boy from the galaxy's outskirts could make himself into a Jedi. Though the extinction of the Jedi had left almost no-one in the universe practising the Force, in principle it remained available to all. This changed with the introduction of midi-chlorians. In *The Phantom Menace*, the Jedi passed from paragons of virtue to freaks of nature. Like a player's avatar in some simplistic video game, one Jedi would be superior to another based on how many midi-chlorian points she had. The analogy to the Christian concepts of salvation and predestination is imperfect but hard to ignore: in the original films, salvation was available to all; in *The Phantom Menace* it was the preserve of an elect few. The effect of this shift in dogma was, in my mind, to dehumanize the Jedi almost entirely. What made Yoda a master was no longer his wisdom, his patience, his determination, or any other virtuous quality of his (as *The Empire Strikes Back* had led me to believe) but merely an excessive presence of microscopic parasites inhabiting his little green body. Seen through the prism of midi-chlorians, Obi-Wan's description of Jedi knights in *Star Wars* as "the guardians of peace and justice in the Old Republic" now seemed rather sinister. I could not help but wonder whether this race of supermen had appointed themselves to their vaunted role.

This second viewing of *The Phantom Menace* proved a turning-point for me. My first viewing left me confused, doubtful and perhaps even in faint denial of what had happened. I looked for some way out of the reality of the situation, namely that George Lucas had made a *Star Wars* film I did not like. Leaving the theatre with Andy on that second night, however, I experienced a glimmer of clarity. *Star Wars* was over for me. It might live on for others—in particular the children Lucas now seemed to be exclusively aiming for—but for me it was passing back into memory. This was nearly the same feeling I had had in the summer of 1991 as I packed away my boxes of toys and memorabilia and prepared for university: fondness for a treasured childhood story now retired to my past. There was one difference now, namely that the new *Star Wars* had sullied my pristine old *Star Wars* in a way that I could not forget. Frustration and disappointment over what might have been now tinged my happy recollections. Retiring to a quiet pub after the film, Andy and I indulged our disgruntlement over *The Phantom Menace* for several pints. It felt good, curative even. But I had no desire to replace my childhood *Star Wars* infatuation with an adulthood *Star Wars* enmity. Brooding would do no good. I had said goodbye to *Star Wars* years ago. The opportunity of welcoming it back like an old friend had gone horribly wrong, but I had to let it go. I had to say goodbye to *Star Wars* again.

*

Mentally, that is precisely what I did. Yet circumstances compelled me to see *The Phantom Menace* two more times. My third viewing occurred when I went home for a brief visit to my mother. She had not seen the film and asked me to go with her. I could not recall my mother ever refusing to take me to see *Star Wars*, so I could hardly fail to return the favour. I spent the better part of the film's running time thinking to myself, *I can't believe I'm seeing this again.* A month or two afterwards, the girl I was dating asked me to take her. I really did not want to go that time, but she was tall and blonde and born in 1980—after *Star Wars*, nearly after *Empire!*—so I agreed. It was a matinee, we were nearly the only people in the theatre, and I fell asleep about two-thirds in. (She thought it was alright. I considered explaining why it was not, but decided against it.)

Lucas made two more prequels, *Attack of the Clones* (2002) and *Revenge of the Sith* (2005). I know I saw them. But in telling contrast to *Star Wars, Empire, Jedi* and even *The Phantom Menace*, I have no specific recollection of going to see either of them. I must have seen them both in Vancouver, for I moved there in the summer of 2001 and, apart from a year-long stint in Ottawa in 2003, have lived and worked there ever since. When *Clones* came out I saw it without enthusiasm and thought it was awful, but beyond that all is blank. My impression of *Revenge of the Sith* was that it was marginally better than the other two prequels, but that is the faintest of praise. (I was—and remain—particularly baffled by the film's howling continuity error: in *Return of the Jedi*, Leia tells Luke that she remembers her mother being "very beautiful" and "kind but sad", while at the end of *Revenge of the Sith* Leia's mother dies in childbirth. This from the same man who re-edited the 2004 DVD release of *The Empire Strikes Back* to dub in a New Zealand accent for Boba Fett.)

Despite this and other grumbles I had about the later two prequels, they faded from my mind almost as soon as they entered it. After the disappointment of *The Phantom Menace* I had made an uneasy peace with the new *Star Wars*. My expectations for the rest of the prequels were subterranean, such that the disappointment they engendered was relatively mild.

Allowing for these two passing exceptions, and also for the six Marvel *Star Wars* comics I framed in glass and hung on the wall of my bachelor pad some time around 2002, the first decade of my twenty-first century was mostly *Star-Wars*-free. I turned thirty, then thirty-five. I worked, fell in love, married, bought a condo, welcomed our first child, sold the condo and bought a house, welcomed our second child, and generally got on with a typical grown-up life.

*

Star Wars marched on without me. Despite the low opinion that I and thousands (millions?) of other thirtysomething men and women had of the prequels, they succeeded in relaunching the *Star Wars* brand. A new generation of children was invited to join the ranks of *Star Wars* fanatics, and a large number seem to have accepted. My sense is that this second wave of *Star Wars* mania was on a smaller scale than what I had known, but I am speculating—the comparative depth of the two phenomena is hard to measure, and in any case I was not paying attention.

Increasingly, however, one did not need to pay attention. With the arrival of the prequels, followed by the *Clone Wars* animated film and television series (neither of which I have ever seen), the early twenty-first century reincarnation of *Star Wars* saturated our popular culture again. Much of this is due, of course, to Lucasfilm's boundless (some would say shameless) devotion to the commercialization of its products. These efforts now went beyond the merchandising and tie-ins with which I was on intimate terms throughout my childhood. In the prequel and post-prequel era, Lucasfilm has become far more willing than previously to hire out *Star Wars* characters as spokesmen (and spokessith and spokesdroids) for other people's products.

Thus in 2010 Darth Vader starred in a Japanese ad campaign for Samsung cellular telephones. Vader's likeness was employed again in early 2011 by Volkswagen to promote its new sedan. Although audience enthusiasm for the dark lord is not restricted to vanquished Axis powers, one might have expected businesses from these particular countries to hesitate somewhat before associating themselves with the most infamous villain in the history of film. Turning to the light side of the Force, Yoda has recently featured in a Japanese commercial for instant soup. He uses his midi-chlorian magic to levitate a giant kettle of boiling water over his own head, then blesses his target market with the words, "May the Force be with Japan". Yoda is also the star, or rather the goat, of a recent UK mobile phone advert in which he accosts a couple in a sushi joint about how to transfer contacts from an old phone to a new one. The attractive young woman looks on incredulously, nearly rolling her eyes at the Jedi master, while the goofy-looking man politely tells him to fuck off. These are only a few examples of George Lucas's distressing willingness, in recent years, to rent out his intellectual properties—who happen to have also been my boyhood icons—to the highest bidder.

Of course if there were no demand for Vaderwagens and Yodafones none of this would happen. The descent of *Star Wars* from modern legend to marketing dreck is a two-way street, and it is not the five-year olds who mistake the prequels for decent films that advertisers are trying to reach by working Yoda into their mobile phone campaigns. My generation participates in the devaluation of *Star Wars* through its tolerance, and even encouragement, of this sort of solicitation. My instinctive reaction is to resent this trivialization of *Star Wars* and its original audience's complicity in it. I must admit, however, that the strength of my response betrays the attachment I still feel to the first three films. Despite all my protestations of having grown out of *Star Wars* and moved on, I am not indifferent to what has become of my childhood fantasy. I don't like seeing *Star Wars* this way.

The obvious solution is not to look. I have already noted that ignoring *Star Wars* is not as easy as it might seem, given the near-constant din of advertising and promotion it generates. But there is a greater problem: children. Were I childless, the unravelling of *Star Wars* at its author's hands would still annoy me, even pain me. But I could disregard it much more easily. The sole reason why *Star Wars* has made yet another sally into my consciousness in recent years is the births of my daughter Beatrice in 2008 and my son Zachary in 2010. Zachary's arrival was more consequential, from a *Star Wars* perspective, than Beatrice's, for I, and much of the rest of the world, still consider *Star Wars* to be chiefly a boy's interest. I acknowledge that this is demonstrably wrong in specific cases, and I certainly have no objection to girls (or women) taking an interest in *Star Wars*. I very much hope Beatrice does like *Star Wars*— by which I mean the real, old, good *Star Wars* of my own childhood and not the broken-down, misconceived *Star Wars* of the moment. Before Zachary's birth, I had given some thought to how I might hide the truth about Darth Vader's relationship with Luke Skywalker from Beatrice until she was old enough for me to show her *The Empire Strikes Back*. I would hate for her to have that film's climax ruined by loose talk on the playground. But no one ever gave my wife and me any hand-me-down, *Star Wars*-emblazoned toddler clothing for Beatrice to wear, and it never occurred to either of us to decorate her room using my framed Marvel *Star Wars* comics. Both these things did happen once we learned that our second child would be a boy. As *Star Wars* made its continued presence felt through my son, I found myself thinking about it more deeply than I ever had. The question was no longer simply, How do I avoid the biggest spoiler in the history of film? I now began to consider the sort of childhood I wanted Zachary to have, and to what extent mine was a good model for it. Of course Zach might turn out a rabid *Star Wars* fan whatever I do. But should I encourage his interest in it at all? The original films were a source of excitement and pleasure for me for years, and the thought of sharing them with my children delights me. But *Star Wars* was not just a film, or even just three films, to me. It was an obsession. I do not say it was a particularly negative obsession. But is obsession ever healthy in a child, whatever it may consist in? Would I not prefer my children to have a wide variety of interests, without single-mindedness about any of them? And if my children are fated to adopt some childhood obsession—and their current infatuation with *Dora the Explorer* and *Go Diego Go!* suggests they may be—should it not be an interest they came to themselves, rather than something their father administered to them like Children's Tylenol?

None of these reservations has prevented Zachary's bedroom décor from taking on a distinctly *Star Wars* theme, but this was not entirely by design—or at least not by my design. It was my wife's idea to dust off my framed Marvel *Star Wars* comics for hanging in the baby's room (once we knew we were expecting a boy). Then, shortly after Zachary's first birthday, my wife suggested I select a few Kenner action figures from my collection for display on a shelf she had cleared for this purpose. I began dreaming up an elaborate diorama of Vader's duel with Obi-Wan, complete with a TIE Fighter in the hangar bay and Luke watching helplessly from afar. Mercifully, my wife shot that idea down. "This is meant to be cool not nerdy", she explained. I opted instead for a simple line-up of ten of the original twelve figures. My wife then combined these with three small, funky robot paintings she had picked up in a local shop. The effect was quite nice, although at this point I was well into work on this book and had begun to have reservations about how much *Star Wars* to cram down my children's throats. But it was only one corner of his room, I told myself. Two months later, on Christmas morning, I helped Zachary open an enormous present. It was a Wampa floor rug from my sister-in-law. I had come across it online while researching this book and pointed it out to my wife only because it was funny. Unbeknownst to me, she decided she liked it and asked her sister to get it for Zachary for Christmas. So now we put our son to bed each night in a *Star Wars* shrine. The poor bastard doesn't stand a chance.

While the Wampa rug was nominally a gift for my one-year-old son, the product itself was surely aimed at my own demographic: aging (and reproducing) *Star Wars* fans. The boys that Lucasfilm and Kenner were forced to give up on around 1985 are now ripe for the picking again. The truth of this was driven home to me about two years ago when, walking past the toy section of a local pharmacy, I saw something I thought I would never see again: *Star Wars* action figures hanging enticingly from wire display racks in the old packaging, the white-and-blue Kenner logo singing out to me from the lower right corner. It was not the sight of *Star Wars* action figures in themselves that struck me. Hasbro (which acquired Kenner in 1991) has been producing figures for years without ever interesting me. What captured my attention this time was the packaging: it was a near perfect imitation of the Kenner blister packs of my childhood.

There was, of course, only one reason to market a new line of *Star Wars* toys this way. Despite the "Ages 4 and up" tagline on the top left corner of every package—exactly where Kenner put it in 1978—the target market for these new toys was not children. It was nostalgic thirty-something suckers like me whose hearts leapt upon seeing Kenner *Star Wars* action figures for sale again. The historical accuracy that has gone into the marketing of these new toys is remarkable. Some of the figures I found hanging from the shelves that day even bore a sticker on the front reading "FREE BOBA FETT" and offering buyers the chance to exchange five proofs-of-purchase for the legendary Rocket Firing Boba Fett action figure—a figure Kenner promised my generation in the late 1970s by means of a similar mail-away offer but never delivered due to last-minute fears about the safety of the rocket. No one under thirty-five would recognize this new promotion for what it was: a nostalgia-laden throwback to our long-gone childhoods. These new toys were not aimed at five-year-olds. They were aimed at their fathers.

I was determined to resist this blatant appeal to my sentimentality. I was thirty-seven years old at the time— too young (I told myself) to feel nostalgic for my lost youth. Besides which, how would I explain to my wife that I had bought a *Star Wars* figure? Yet every subsequent trip to the pharmacy—and later to the grocery store, which also began to stock the things— was a temptation. I kept wandering into the toy section, just to have a look. Eventually I learned all about this new line of *Star Wars* action figures from the internet. Hasbro is behind it, of course; Kenner has been dead for years. Furthermore, in a stroke of evil genius, Hasbro was anachronistically marketing characters from all six *Star Wars* films in this Kenner style, a ploy that, when I first saw it in person at the grocery store, momentarily ingratiated me to the prequels. I got over that almost immediately but the fact that it happened at all is incredible.

I eventually admitted to myself that I was going to buy one of these new "Kenner" figurines. It was, as the man said, useless to resist. I decided upon Rebel Fleet Trooper, nearly the first character the audience sees in *Star Wars* yet a figure which for some reason the real Kenner never produced. I had seen Rebel Fleet Trooper on a web site but could never find it at the grocery store. I even made a furtive trip to a real toy shop once, but still could not find it. I learned that the figure was rare and was selling online at twice its retail price or more. I lost my patience. While picking up cold medicine for my daughter at the downtown London Drugs, I grabbed a Luke Skywalker (Jedi Knight) from the store's small toy section and hoped the cashier would not ask me why. She didn't. I stuffed the contraband into my laptop bag and left it there overnight so that my wife would not see. She probably would have only laughed a little, but I was embarrassed and did not want to have to explain. I did not really know what the explanation was.

When I got to work the next morning I closed the door to my office, pulled out the hidden figurine and admired it in its packaging. I briefly contemplated leaving it there, unopened, "mint-in-box", as the collectors say. But that would only make a silly situation sillier. So I tore the plastic from the cardback and, after quite a struggle—these new figures are very securely packaged—extracted Luke and his accessories. The likeness was very good, better even than in Kenner's best work. Furthermore, the figure had joints everywhere: shoulders, elbows, wrists, waist, knees, even ankles—a complete contrast with Kenner's figures, which could only march straight-armed and straight-legged like toy soldiers (which is, after all, what they were).

But there was something off about this figure. What it gained in articulation and likeness it lost in playability. I could not imagine my children, or anyone's children, playing with the thing. It was too dainty. The hundred or so real Kenner action figures packed securely in their Kenner carrying cases in my basement storage closet had been subjected to hundreds of hours of punishing play, yet most were intact and even well-preserved. Their thick hands and inflexible limbs made them durable. This new figure, however attractive, felt fragile. It was not so much an action figure as an inaction figure, suitable for display only. I should not have been surprised. To convince a 37-year-old man to buy an action figure was already an accomplishment on Hasbro's part. To persuade him to play with it would be a perverse sort of miracle. Just as Hasbro did not intend to sell these figures to children, it did not intend that anyone actually play with them. I certainly did not buy Luke Skywalker (Jedi Knight) to play with it. I bought it out of sentimentality. For that purpose—if sentimentality is a purpose—these new Kenner/Hasbro figures, or at least those derived from the original trilogy, are very apt. But they are not really toys.

My Luke Skywalker (Jedi Knight) now lives in the top drawer of my desk at work, surrounded by business cards, paper clips and boxes of staples. He has some company. I broke down again and bought Darth Vader as a supposed first birthday gift for Zachary, but it turned out to be more intricate and fragile even than Skywalker—its tiny helmet comes in two parts and is always falling off—so I brought it to work, too. I never have found a Rebel Fleet Trooper.

Despite these lapses into nostalgia, and the immersion in *Star Wars* demanded by writing this book, I am, for the most part, only a distant observer of today's *Star Wars*. Recently at work I was chatting with two colleagues about our young children's pop culture interests. The mum said her three-year-old son was crazy about the movie *Cars*. I mentioned that Beatrice loves *Go Diego Go*. The other dad then told a story about how his son had demanded that his father buy him a pair of Commander Cody shoes.

"Who's Commander Cody?", I said innocently. The other dad, an old-time *Star Wars* fan who shares my distaste for the prequels, explained that Commander Cody is a character in the *Clone Wars* television series, and possibly also in one of the prequels. It was the first time in my entire life that someone had made a *Star Wars* reference I did not get. My initial reaction was mild amazement. Then I began to feel rather pleased with myself. *This really is over*, I thought. *Star Wars used to be mine, and now it is not. I'm okay with that.*

INVENT ME A STORY

"Papa, I want you to invent me a story." The lights are out in Beatrice's room. She is tucked in almost to her nose. Most nights I read her stories from the dozens of books on her shelf, nestled in bed with her, the reading light over her left shoulder. But sometimes Beatrice wants me to "invent" her a story. This is easier some nights than others. Tonight it is not easy. I have had a long day at work, and the Canucks game is beckoning in the living room. I decide, just this once, to take a shortcut.

"Once upon a time there was a princess who wore a white gown…"

"Like Snow White, uh?" ("Uh?" is Beatrice's French-Canadian way of saying "Eh?" or "Right?" or "N'est-ce pas?". We speak mostly French at home—my wife is

141

from New Brunswick—and Beatrice's English carries a diminishing, but still pronounced, French accent.)

"A little. But this princess has a very important message, a secret message, that she is hiding from an evil king."

Beatrice lets out a thrilled gasp. "And he has a sword, uh? To make people dead?"

"Yes, a red sword. And he wears all black robes. His name is Vader. One day, Vader captures the princess's spaceship. (This princess has a spaceship.) The princess has to act quickly. She gives her secret message to a little blue robot named Artoo and tells him to give it to a wise old man named Ben. Then Artoo and his friend Threepio, who is a tall, gold robot, escape in a tiny ship and fly away."

"Threepio?" Beatrice interjects. "That's a good name. But what's the message?"

"It explains how to destroy the bad king's fortress."

"So he can't make people dead anymore?"

"Right. So off go the robots to a faraway planet that is all desert…"

"With camels and cactuses and crocodiles?"

"And big lizards, too. So the robots land in the desert and Artoo tries to go find Ben…"

"Ben's a bad king, uh?"

"No no, Ben's a wise old man who can help the princess. He…"

"With a sword to make people dead?"

"Well, he has a sword, but it's blue, and it's to protect people from the bad king Vader. Shall I go on?" Beatrice nods.

"Artoo and Threepio get lost in the desert and, when the night falls, they are captured by little dwarves in brown coats."

"Like in *Snow White*."

"Sort of, but these dwarves say, 'Achkeba chegabada utini!'" Beatrice laughs. "The dwarves collect robots and sell them to people. In the morning, they set up their market and put Artoo and Threepio up for sale. A man—more like a boy, really—comes to the market to buy some robots. His name is Skywalker."

Beatrice gives a drawn-out, "Oh". She now understands that this is a Skywalker story. I am afraid she will accuse me (rightly) of not really inventing a story, but she is sufficiently intrigued to let me go on.

"Skywalker buys the tall gold robot, and also a little red one. This makes Artoo sad, because he wants to stay with his friend Threepio. Just then the red robot explodes!"

"Why?" asks Beatrice.

"I don't know. It was broken. So Skywalker takes the little blue one instead, and Threepio and Artoo are together again. Later…"

"And they're happy to be back together, uh?" Beatrice is showing me that she is following along.

"Later, Skywalker is cleaning up Artoo when he comes across the princess's message! It shoots out of the robot like light from a flashlight. Skywalker sees the princess saying, 'Help me, Ben, help me! The evil king has captured me.'"

"Ben is the evil king, uh?"

"No no, Ben is the princess's friend. Vader is the evil king. He wears all black. Skywalker thinks the princess is beautiful. He wants to know why she needs help. But Artoo won't tell him! He says the message is a secret. That night, when everyone is asleep, Artoo runs away from Skywalker to go find Ben."

I pause, running my hand through Beatrice's hair. "It's time for bed now. I'll tell you the rest of the story tomorrow."

"Tomorrow at breakfast, okay?"

I equivocate, then sing Beatrice *My Funny Valentine*, watching as her head tilts back, mouth open, eyes closed. When I am certain she has fallen asleep, I climb carefully out of her bed and tiptoe to the door. I grasp the doorknob firmly to keep it from rattling, then slowly turn it. When the latch is fully retracted, I swing the door open just wide enough to pass through, letting as little light into her room as possible as I step into the hallway. I draw back the door, placing my fingers in the frame to dampen the sound, and prepare to turn the knob gently from the outside.

There is a rustle from Beatrice's bed. I've blown it.

"Papa?" says Beatrice. I re-open the door enough to peer inside.

"Yes?"

"It's a good story, uh?"

ABOUT THE AUTHOR

Gib van Ert lives in Vancouver, British Columbia with his wife and two children. He is a lawyer and the author of *Using International Law in Canadian Courts* and other serious legal works that have nothing to do with *Star Wars*. He had hoped to use the revenue from this book to pay off his remaining student debt before turning 40. So much for that. Lately he has been blogging about *Star Wars* at http://thissortofthing.com.

A REQUEST

Please consider reviewing this book on Amazon, Goodreads, Facebook, Twitter, your blog or elsewhere. Your comments are valuable to me and may help readers learn about my book. Thanks!

Printed in Great Britain
by Amazon.co.uk, Ltd.,
Marston Gate.